AF600426

THE MINISTER OF THE LAST SACRAMENTS

The Catholic University of America
Canon Law Studies
No. 299

The Minister of the Last Sacraments

A DISSERTATION

SUBMITTED TO THE FACULTY OF THE SCHOOL OF CANON LAW OF THE CATHOLIC UNIVERSITY OF AMERICA IN PARTIAL FULFILLMENT OF THE REQUIREMENTS FOR THE DEGREE OF DOCTOR OF CANON LAW

BY THE
REVEREND FRANCIS J. STATKUS, J.C.L.
Priest of the Archdiocese of Philadelphia

The Catholic University of America Press
Washington, D. C.
1951

NIHIL OBSTAT:

CLEMENS V. BASTNAGEL, S.T.L., J.U.D.

Censor Deputatus

Washingtonii, D. C., die 24 novembris, 1950

IMPRIMATUR:

✠ D. CARD. DOUGHERTY

Archiepiscopus Philadelphiensis

Philadelphiae, die 28 novembris, 1950.

MURRAY & HEISTER
WASHINGTON, D. C.

PRINTED BY
TIMES AND NEWS PUBLISHING CO.
GETTYSBURG, PA., U. S. A.

TO MY
MOTHER AND FATHER

FOREWORD

It will be the purpose of this dissertation to examine in detail who according to law is the exclusive minister of the last sacraments, and the certain exclusive prerogatives which have been accorded by law to the minister. The work will be restricted to the ministry of the last sacraments to dying Catholics. Consequently the ministry of the sacrament of baptism will be completely omitted, although to a dying unbaptized person baptism would be considered a last sacrament. The dissertation will treat in some substantial although imperfect manner of the ministry of last confession, Holy Viaticum, and extreme unction.

An effort will be made to determine both the right and the obligation of the minister to administer these sacraments so vitally important at the moment of death.

The writer takes this occasion to express his sincere gratitude to His Eminence, Dennis Cardinal Dougherty, Archbishop of Philadelphia, for the opportunity to pursue advanced studies in Canon Law; to the Faculty of the School of Canon Law at the Catholic University of America, Washington, D. C., for their kind guidance and assistance; and to all others who have aided in any way in the preparation of this work.

TABLE OF CONTENTS

TABLE OF CONTENTS (Continued)

TABLE OF CONTENTS (Continued)

PART ONE

Historical Synopsis

CHAPTER I

The Minister of the Last Sacraments From the First Centuries to the Council of Trent (1545-1563)

ARTICLE 1. THE MINISTER OF LAST CONFESSION

Section 1. The Priest

A. From the First Centuries to the *Decree* of Gratian (ca. 1140)

The bishop alone was the ordinary minister of both public and private confession for at least the first four centuries.[1] However, decrees of early councils as well as the writings of the early Fathers reveal that the bishop delegated the priest to be the minister of confession for the sick and also in cases of urgent necessity.

The *Decree* of Gratian contained a spurious text of Pope Evaristus (99-107) declaring that priests with the bishop's permission should reconcile penitents guilty of occult sins, and that the priests should likewise absolve and communicate the sick. It appears from the text that the bishop's permission was not necessary in the priests' service of the sick.[2]

[1] Vacandard, "Confession du Ier in XIIIe Siècle," *Dictionnaire de Theologie Catholique* (14 vols. in 23, Paris, 1903-1939), III, 840-844 (hereafter cited as *DTC*); Tanquerey, *Synopsis Theologiae Dogmaticae* (24. ed., 3 vols., Parisiis: Desclée et Socii, 1938), III, 49; Marténe, *De Antiquis Ecclesiae Ritibus Libri Quattuor* (4 vols., Rotomagi, 1700-1706), Lib. I, pars II, cap. 6, art. 6-Vol. I, 34.

[2] "Presbiteri de occultis peccatis iussione episcopi penitentes reconcilient, et, sicut supra permisimus, infirmantes absolvant et communicent."—*Corpus Iuris Canonici* (Editio Lipsiensis II [Richter-Friedberg] 2 vols., Lipsiae, 1879-1881), c. 4, C. XXVI, q. 6; Jaffé, *Regesta Pontificum Romanorum ab condita Ecclesia ad annum post Christum natum MCXCVIII* (editionem 2. correctam et auctam auspiciis Gulielmi Wattenbach, curaverunt F. Kaltenbrunner, P. Ewald, S. Loewenfeld, 2 vols. in 1, Lipsiae, 1885-1888), n. 125 (hereafter cited as Jaffé); Mansi, *Sacrorum Conciliorum Nova et Amplissima Collectio* (53 vols. in 60, Parisiis, 1901-1927), I, 632 (hereafter cited as Mansi).

St. Cyprian (ca. 210-258) wrote that persons afflicted with some illness or otherwise incommoded were to make their confession to a priest, if a bishop could not be had. And if death was imminent, and a priest was not available, then the sick persons were to confess to a deacon, in order that after the imposition of hands the dying persons might regain union with God.[3]

The thirty-second canon of the Council of Elvira (ca. 305) according to many authors granted priests the power of reconciling excommunicates who were overtaken by a perilous illness.[4]

Another spurious text, which was attributed to Pope St. Julius I (337-352), stated that the priest was responsible for those souls to whom he denied penance at the moment of death. Gratian's *Decree* likewise incorporated this statement.[5]

St. Ambrose (340-397) in treating of penance stated that the *sacerdos* was the judge, and that Christ granted to him alone the right of loosing and binding. Excerpts of his writings were incorporated into the *Decree* of Gratian.[6]

Vacandard (1849-1927), however, claimed that the word *sacerdos* before the fifth century very rarely applied to a priest, and least of all in reference to the ministry of confession. He stated that *sacerdos* almost always referred to the bishop.[7]

In 390 the II Council of Carthage legislated that the priest was to consult the bishop before reconciling one whose life was imperiled. Such action in the granting of reconciliation was allowed only when the bishop was not available.[8]

---

[3] Epist. XII, n. 1:—Migne, *Patrologiae Cursus Completus, Series Latina* (221 vols., Parisiis, 1844-1864), IV, 259 (hereafter cited as *MPL*).

[4] Cf. *infra*, pp. 15-16.

[5] "Si presbiter penitentiam abnegaverit morientibus, reus erit animarum . . ."—c. 12, C. XXVI, q. 6; Jaffé, n. 211; Mansi, II, 1266.

[6] Cf. *De Poenitentia*, Lib. I, c. 2-c. 51, D. I, *de poenit.; De Cain et Abel*, Lib. II, c. 4-c. 78, D. I, *de poenit.*

[7] Cf. "Confession du Ier au XIIIe Siècle," *DTC*, III, 844.

[8] Can. 4: "Si quisquam in periculo fuerit constitutus, et se reconciliari diurnis altaribus petierit, si episcopus absens fuerit, debet utique presbiter consulere episcopum, et sic periclitantem eius precepto reconciliare. Quam rem debemus salubri consilio roborare."—c. 5, C. XXVI, q. 6; Bruns, *Canones Apostolorum et Conciliorum Saeculorum IV, V, VI, VII* (2 vols., Berolini, 1839), I, 119 (hereafter cited as Bruns); Mansi, III, 869.

In commenting on this text as it was incorporated in Gratian's *Decree,* the *Glossa Ordinaria* stated that this legislation referred to those penitents who were excommunicated by the bishop or who had received their penance from him.[9]

The thirtieth canon of the Council of Hippo (393) stated that the bishop was the ordinary minister of reconciliation, and the priest the delegated minister.[10] The III Council of Carthage (397) explicitly legislated that in a case of urgent necessity the priest could reconcile a penitent without even consulting the bishop.[11] Again, in 398 the IV Council of Carthage spoke of the priest as administering penance and reconciling the seriously ill person. No mention was made of episcopal delegation.[12]

From the foregoing it is manifest that for the first four centuries the bishop was the ordinary minister of confession, but that in a case of urgent necessity the priest could grant reconciliation. Usually, however, episcopal permission was needed if the priest was to act with the proper authorization.

In the subsequent centuries the testimony of the councils and of the writers abounded with information to show that the priest began more and more to exercise the ministry not only of last confession, but also of ordinary confession.[13] However, Vacandard stated that even during the fifth century the intervention of the priest in penitential matters called for a previous episcopal delegation.[14]

Venerable Bede (673-735) remarked that the spiritual head of the Christian community in Ireland was a priest, and that he exercised jurisdiction even over the bishops. This arrangement, he stated, existed during St. Columban's times (ca. 530-615).[15]

[9] Ad c. 5, C. XXVI, q. 6, s. v. *Si episcopus.*

[10] Bruns, I, 137.

[11] Can. 32: "Inconsulto episcopo poenitentem presbiter non reconciliet, nisi ultima cogat necessitas."—c. 14, C. XXVI, q. 6; Bruns, I, 127; Mansi, III, 885.

[12] Can. 76. Cf. c. 8, C. XXVI, q. 6; Bruns, I, 148; Mansi, III, 957.

[13] Cf. St. Jerome, *In Matth.*, XVI, 19—*MPL,* XXVI, 118; III Council of Toledo (589), cans. 11-12—Mansi, IX, 995.

[14] Cf. "Confession du Ier au XIIIe Siècle," *DTC,* III, 874.

[15] *Historia Ecclesiastica Gentis Anglorum,* Litt. III, cap. 4: "Habere autem solet ipsa insula rectorem semper abbatem presbyterum, cujus juri et omnis

Vacandard inferred from this text that in Ireland priests were the ordinary ministers of confession as well as of last confession.[16]

Further evidence was furnished in the seventh century by Theodore, Bishop of Canterbury (+ 690), who in speaking of confessors did not distinguish between the rights of a bishop and a priest.[17]

Conciliar enactments, diocesan statutes and various writings of the eighth and ninth centuries throughout Western Europe stated so explicitly that the priest should minister the sacrament of penance to the sick and the dying faithful that as a result no doubt remained of the priest's function in the capacity of ordinary minister. The following testified to that fact: The twentieth sacerdotal right as listed in the *Excerpts of Egbert* (748), Archbishop of York (735-766);[18] the Capitulary of Theodulf (+ 821) for his priests in 798;[19] Jonas, Bishop of Orleans (818-843);[20] the Council of Aachen (836);[21] the Council of Mainz (847);[22] and the Council of Pavia (850).[23]

When writing about confession in general, Alcuin (735-804) recalled to the faithful the obligation of confessing to priests,[24] and the Council of Anse (990) distinguished between confession as made to God and as made to priests.[25]

The non-continuance of the bishop's administration of penance as its exclusive minister was in all likelihood occasioned by the

---

provincia et ipsi etiam episcopi, ordine inusitato debeant esse subjecti juxta exemplum primi doctoris illius, qui non Episcopus, sed Presbyter extitit et monachus."—*MPL,* XCV, 122.

[16] Cf. "Confession du Ier au XIIIe Siècle," *DTC,* III, 874.

[17] *Poenitentiale,* cap. 31—*MPL,* XCIX, 946.

[18] Mansi, XII, 415; *MPL,* LXXXIX, 382 ff.

[19] Mansi, XIII, n. 5, 996; *MPL,* CV, 220.

[20] *Institutio Laicalis,* Lib. III, c. 12—*MPL,* CV, 260-261.

[21] *De Vita et Doctrina Inferiorum Ordinum,* cap. 5—*Monumenta Germaniae Historica,* Legum Sectio III, *Concilia,* tom. II, pars II (ed. A. Werminghoff, Hannoverae et Lipsiae, 1908), 711-712 (hereafter cited as *MGH*); Hardouin, *Acta Conciliorum et Epistolae Decretales ac Constitutiones Summorum Pontificum* (12 vols., Parisiis, 1714-1715), IV, 1397 (hereafter cited as Hardouin).

[22] Can. 23. Cf. c. 1, C. XXVI, q. 7; Hardouin, V, 13; Mansi, XIV, 910.

[23] Cap. 8—Hardouin, V, 27.

[24] *Epist. CXII—MPL,* C. 337.

[25] Cap. 30—Mansi, XIX, 188.

growth in the number of the faithful. Conversions became more numerous; parishes were established, and the number of Catholics increased to such proportions that the bishop alone could not cope with the needed administration of the sacrament of penance. He needed the assistance of the parish priests. The fact also that public confession became more rare enhanced the position of the priest as the minister of private confession.

The *Liber de Vera et Falsa Penitentia*, a twelfth century work falsely attributed to St. Augustine (354-430), and cited by Gratian (+ ca. 1157), Peter Lombard (+ ca. 1160), Alain de Lille (+ 1202), and others, mentioned the priest as the minister of penance.[26]

This work was important for the fact also that it advocated lay confession. And many who advocated lay confessions looked to this work in warrant of their doctrine.

B. From the *Decree* of Gratian (ca. 1140) to the Council of Trent (1545-1563)

It is not known for a certainty whether Gratian himself believed that confession was necessary for sacramental penance. As for the priest being its minister, Gratian at best quoted early writers and councils which explicitly mentioned the bishops and priests as ministers of confession. These texts of the early Fathers and the enactments of the early councils have all been cited in chronological order in the preceding pages. At best, from these writings as found in the *Decree* of Gratian one can only infer that Gratian himself probably believed that the priest was the ordinary minister of regular confession as well as of last confession.[27]

It should be noted here too that the *Decree* of Gratian contained texts of writers advocating lay confession.[28] Two of the

---

[26] Cap. 10. "Qui vult confiteri peccata, ut inveniat gratiam, quaerat sacerdotem qui sciat ligare et solvere."—c. 88, D. I, *de poenit.; MPL*, XL, 1113.

[27] Cf. c. 51, D. I, *de poenit.;* cc. 4, 5, 8, 12, 14, C. XXVI, q. 6.

[28] *Liber de Vera et Falsa Penitentia*, cap. 10—c. 88, D. I, *de poenit.; Epistola ad Fortunatum*: "Nam cum illa historia narratur, omnes, qui audiunt, ad lacrimas moventur. Cum in navi quadam nullus fidelis esset praeter unum penitentem, cepit imminere naufragium. Erat ibi quidam non

passages were drawn from pseudo-Augustinian works. Concerning the second of these as here reproduced, much doubt exists regarding its possible intent to include also the consideration of lay confession. The *Glossa Ordinaria* subscribed to the view that the text advocated a lay minister to hear the confession in a case of urgent necessity.[29] Laurain held the same opinion.[30] Teetaert, however, claims that with this text Gratian intended simply to show that baptism when administered by a lay person was valid, and that he did not propose to insinuate any further conclusions.[31]

The IV General Council of the Lateran (1215) not only legislated that the priest was the ordinary minister of confession, but it also obligated the faithful to confess at least once a year (at Paschal time) to their own priest. Furthermore the Council added that if anyone wished to confess to another priest for some just cause, then such a person should seek and obtain the permission of the proper priest, otherwise the absolution would be invalid. This enactment became incorporated in the Decretals of Pope Gregory IX (1234).[32]

Later writers used this text consistently for proving that the proper priest alone could offer the benefit of the penitential forum for his subjects. Of the later writers Hostiensis and St. Raymond of Pennafort seemed to treat the ministry of penance in detail, and practically all the other commentators followed their teaching.

Hostiensis (+ 1271) stressed the fact that mortal sins had to be confessed to the parochial priest, who was given power by the

immemor suae salutis, et sacramenti vehentissimus flagitator, nec erat aliquis, qui dare posset, nisi penitens ille; acceperat enim, pro peccato, de quo agebat penitentiam, amiserat sanctitatem, sed non amiserat sacramentum. Nam si hoc amittunt peccantes, cum reconciliantur post penitentiam, quare non iterum baptizantur? Dedit ergo quod acceperat, et, ne periculose vitam finiret non reconciliatus, petiit ab eo ipso, quem baptizaverat, ut eum reconciliaret, et factum est: evaserunt naufragium." Cf. c. 36, D. IV, *de cons.* (This canon bears the superscription: *Valet baptisma, etsi per laicos ministretur.*)

[29] Ad c. 1, C. XVI, q. 1, s. v. *sepeliat.*

[30] *De l'Intervention des Laïques, des Diacres et des Abbesses dans l'Administration de la Pénitence* (Paris, 1897), p. 207.

[31] *La Confession aux Laïques dans l'Eglise Latine depuis le VIIIe Siècle jusqu' au XIVe* (Paris, 1926), p. 207.

[32] Can. 21—c. 12, X, *de poenitentiis et remissionibus,* V, 38.

bishop to hear the confessions of his parishioners. However, he made several exceptions to this general rule, among which was the case of necessity. With reference to this exceptional case he asserted that the efficacy of confession was so great that in the absence of the parochial priest, or also of any other priest, the person pressed by necessity could confess to a layman or even to a laywoman, if a man was not available. A case of necessity was verified when there was either a danger of death or a departure for war. If the person recovered from his illness or returned from the war, then he was obliged to confess to his own parochial priest. Hostiensis insisted, however, that even in a time of necessity a person could not confess to a heretic or to a schismatic, since such a person was not a keeper of the keys of heaven. Excommunicates, unless they were bound by only a minor excommunication, could likewise not absolve. Only the penance which was administered by a priest was sacramental in its character.[33]

St. Raymond of Pennafort (ca. 1175-1275) proposed the following views:

1. Everyone has to confess to a priest to whom the Lord had given the power of binding and loosing.

2. Not every priest can hear confessions, for though it is to be admitted that every priest at ordination receives the power of the keys, yet he cannot use that power without the necessary jurisdiction that must be granted by the diocesan bishop or the Holy See.

3. The faithful are held to confess to their proper priests, under whose care the bishop has placed them. Only with the consent of the proper priest, or for a reasonable cause, could a penitent confess to another priest.

4. *In articulo necessitatis* the penitent could confess to any priest available, provided that the priest is not a heretic, schismatic, or an excommunicate. In the absence of a priest the person who is afflicted with an illness or is about to enter a just war can confess not only to a cleric, but even to his neighbor, a lay person. Confes-

[33] *Summa Aurea* (Lugduni, 1568), Lib. V, *de poenitentiis et remissionibus*, p. 410.

sion to a non-sacerdotal cleric or to a lay person, according to St. Raymond, was not *de precepto.*[34]

Finally, in the fifteenth century the practice of lay confession was explicitly condemned by means of a series of decrees issued by the Roman Pontiffs, and the right of hearing confessions was vindicated solely to the priests.

Pope Martin V (1417-1431), in the twentieth test question of the Bull *Inter cunctas,* questioned the adherents of Wycliff and Huss who firmly believed in lay confession. He expressly condemned lay confessions.[35]

Pope Eugene IV (1431-1447) in an Instruction to the Armenians expressed even more definitely that the minister of confession was a priest.[36] And Leo X (1513-1521) in the Bull *Exsurge Domine* condemned the practice of lay confession.[37]

Section 2. Other Ministers

A. The Deacons

As early as the third century history bore testimony to the fact that the deacons heard confessions. St. Cyprian (ca. 210-258) wrote that, if a bishop or a priest was not available to a person who was afflicted with illness or who was otherwise straitened, then the penitent was to confess his sins to a deacon.[38] And according to some writers the disputed thirty-second canon of the Council

[34] Cf. *Summa Sancti Raymundi de Pennafort* (Veronae, 1744), Lib. III, tit. 34, *de poenitentiis et remissionibus,* pp. 423-426.

[35] Const. *Inter cunctas,* 22 febr. 1418: "Utrum credat quod christianus ultra contritionem cordis, habita copia sacerdotis idonei, soli sacerdoti de necessitate salutis confiteri teneatur, et non laico seu laicis, quantumcumque bonis et devotis."—Denzinger, Bannwart, et Umberg, *Enchiridion Symbolorum, Definitionum, et Declarationum de Rebus Fidei et Morum* (21.-23. ed., Friburgi Brisgoviae: Herder & Co., 1937), p. 327, n. 929 (hereafter cited as *Enchiridion*); *Codicis Iuris Canonici Fontes,* cura Emi Petri Card. Gasparri editi (9 vols., Romae, 1923-1939), (Vols. VII-IX, ed. cura et studio Emi Iustiniani Card. Serédi), n. 43 (hereafter cited *Fontes*).

[36] Const. *Exultate Deo,* 22 nov. 1439—Denzinger, *Enchiridion,* n. 699; *Fontes,* n. 52.

[37] 16 maii 1520, I, n. 13—Denzinger, *Enchiridion,* n. 741; *Fontes,* n. 76.

[38] *Epistola XII,* n. 1—*MPL,* IV, 259.

of Elvira (ca. 305) granted to the deacons the permission of hearing the confessions of those who were in urgent need of a confessor.[39]

It was from the ninth to the thirteenth centuries that the practice of the deacons' hearing of confessions became a common practice. During that time the deacons heard confessions not only in cases of urgent necessity, but at times also under ordinary circumstances.[40] The deacons' participation in penitential matters became such an abuse that as a consequence various councils enacted legislation which prohibited the deacons from hearing confessions or imposing penance except in cases of grave necessity.[41]

In the year 1280 the Synod of Poitiers threatened excommunication to every deacon who heard confessions or absolved sinners. The synod stated that deacons could not absolve, since they did not have the power of the keys which the priests alone possessed.[42] From about that time onward no testimony exists regarding the deacons' continued practice of hearing confessions; thus the practice seems to have been uprooted in the latter part of the thirteenth century.

The reader must be reminded not only with reference to the deacons but also in relation to all others who were not priests that they could never absolve sinners from their sins. An ill person, or a person finding himself in some case of urgent necessity, was exhorted to confess his sins in the absence of a priest to a deacon, or to a minor cleric, or even to a lay person, in order that a greater sorrow would be aroused within the penitent, which sorrow might never have been achieved if the penitent had not confessed to someone.

---

[39] Cf. *infra*, pp. 15-16.

[40] Cf. Etienne, Bishop of Autun (1112-1139), *De Sacramento Altaris*, c. 7—*MPL*, CLXX, 1279; Council of Tribur (895), cap. 31—Mansi, XVIII, 148.

[41] Council of York (1195), can. 6—Mansi, XXII, 653; *Synodicae Constitutiones* (1197) of Eudes of Sully, Archbishop of Paris (1196-1208), can. 56—Mansi, XXII, 676; Council of London (1200), can. 3—Mansi, XXII, 714; Council of Rouen (1231), can. 34—Mansi, XXIII, 218; Council of Worcester (1240), can. 26—Mansi, XXIII, 535.

[42] Cap. 5—Mansi, XXIV, 383-384; Hardouin, VI, 853.

B. The Charismatics and Women Confessors

Charismatics, a group of persons favored with particular graces, exercised some authority in penitential matters. However, they served more as directors of consciences rather than as absolvers of sins. This practice prevailed particularly in the first four centuries.[43]

Particularly from the seventh until the thirteenth century history reveals the fact that religious superioresses or abbesses assumed the right to hear the faults of their subjects by way of confession. In the year 1210 Pope Innocent III in an epistle to the bishops of Burgos and Valencia and to the abbot of the monastery of Morimond forbade the superioresses to hear the confessions of their subjects.[44]

C. The Monks

It appeared to be the general rule for monks to feel obliged to confess to their own abbots or to some priest delegated by the abbot. This general rule applied practically to all the monasteries until the thirteenth century. An exception was made but very rarely, e.g., the constitutions of the monastery of Cluny, France, permitted its monks to choose the prior rather than the abbot for confession when they were near death.[45]

The thirteenth century was of quite some importance in the development of confessional discipline in the monasteries. During this century the Mendicant Orders of Friars received through their approved constitutions the privilege of confessing to any priest of the Order, or, if that was impossible, to any other discreet priest.

---

[43] Cf. Vacandard, "Confession du Ier au XIIIe Siècle," *DTC,* III, 847-848, 875.

[44] Potthast, *Regesta Pontificum Romanorum inde ab anno post Christum natum MCXCVIII ad annum MCCCIV* (2 vols., Berolini, 1874-1875), n. 4143 (hereafter cited as Potthast) ; c. 10, X, *de poenitentiis et remissionibus,* V, 38; cf. Vacandard, "Confession du Ier au XIIIe Siècle," *DTC,* III, 879.

[45] *Udalrici Consuetudines Cluniacenses,* Lib. II, c. 26—*MPL,* CXCLIX, 712; cf. McCormick, *Confessors of Religious,* The Catholic University of America Canon Law Studies, n. 33 (Washington, D. C.: The Catholic University of America, 1926), pp. 1-17.

Hence, the friars enjoyed also the freedom of choosing their own confessor at the moment of death.[46]

To the monks' right of exercising parochial duties outside of their monasteries Gratian devoted the first *quaestio* of *Causa XVI* of his *Decretum*. It appears from Gratian's treatment of the matter that the monks could impose penance, could baptize, and could administer also other priestly duties; but the free selection of them by the people, the bishop's authorization, and also the abbot's consent were prerequired factors for the exercise of these sacramental functions. Thus these conditions, it seems, had to be fulfilled before a monk could hear a last confession of a lay person.[47]

In the thirteenth century Boniface VIII (1294-1303) granted to the Mendicants the privilege of hearing the confessions of the laity. This privilege allowed the Mendicants even to enter the home of a sick person for the sake of hearing his confession. The confessor, however, had to be asked for; he could not volunteer his services without being asked. This privilege was communicated also to the other religious, and other Pontiffs granted similar privileges to other Orders.[48]

Nuns ordinarily confessed to a confessor general, whose status was similar to that of the present day ordinary confessor of nuns. To him also the nuns customarily made their last confession. The confessor general was either the abbot of the Order to which also the nuns belonged, or he was appointed to that office after being elected to it by the entire community.[49]

ARTICLE 2. THE MINISTER OF HOLY VIATICUM

Section 1. From the First Centuries to the Decree of Gratian

A pseudo-Isidorian decree, attributed to Pope Evaristus (97-105), stated that priests should reconcile penitents guilty of occult sins, and that they should absolve and communicate the sick. The

[46] Cf. McCormick, *ibid.*, p. 13.

[47] Cf. *Dictum*, p. c. 25, C. XVI, q. 1.

[48] Cf. c. 2, *de sepulturis*, III, 7, in Clem.; cf. McCormick, *Confessors of Religious*, p. 16.

[49] Cf. McCormick, *op. cit.*, pp. 75-82.

bishop's order or consent was needed for the reconciliation of penitents guilty of occult sins, but for the care of the sick no consent appeared to be necessary. This decree was incorporated into Gratian's collection.[50]

Tertullian (ca. 160-ca. 235), writing during the Roman persecutions, mentioned in a letter to his wife the fact that the faithful carried the Holy Eucharist to their homes and received the Sacrament there.[51] Reservation of the Blessed Sacrament in homes was again alluded to in another of Tertullian's works.[52]

St. Cyprian (ca. 210-258) forbade the *lapsi* to communicate themselves from their household repositories.[53] St. Ambrose (340-397) narrated that Holy Communion was put in possession of sea travelers, so that in the case of a shipwreck they would not die without Holy Communion.[54] St. Basil (329-379) related that in Alexandria everyone kept the Holy Eucharist in his home, and that whenever anyone wished to communicate himself he did so.[55]

From the writings of these Fathers it can be concluded that at least during emergencies the laity ministered the Blessed Sacrament to others and to themselves. St. Basil appears to give evidence that the laity were ministers even under ordinary circumstances.[56]

St. Dionysius, Bishop of Alexandria (ca. 247-265), in a letter to Fabius, Bishop of Antioch (250-252), related how Serapion, an infirm old man, received Viaticum from his grandchild, who in turn had received the consecrated particle from a priest. The priest

---

[50] "Presbiteri de occultis peccatis iussione episcopi penitentes reconcilient, et, sicut supra praemisimus, infirmantes absolvant et communicent."—c. 4, C. XXVI, q. 6; Jaffé, n. 125.

[51] *Ad Uxorem,* Lib. II, cap. 5—*MPL,* I, 1296.

[52] *De Oratione,* n. 19—*Corpus Scriptorum Ecclesiasticorum Latinorum* (Vindobonae: F. Tempsky, 1866-), Vol. XX (ed. Reifferscheid et Wissowa, 1890), 192 (hereafter cited as *CSEL*) ; *MPL,* I, 1181.

[53] *De Lapsis,* n. 26—*MPL,* IV, 486-487; *CSEL,* III, pars I, 256.

[54] *De Excessu Fratris sui Satyri,* Lib. I, n. 43—*MPL,* XVI, 1304.

[55] Epist. XCIII—Migne, *Patrologiae Cursus Completus, Series Graeca* (161 vols., Parisiis, 1856-1866), XXXII, 486 (hereafter cited as *MPG*).

[56] Cf. Dublanchy, "Viaticum," *DTC,* III, 491-492; De Augustinis, *De Re Sacramentaria* (4 vols. in 2, Woodstock, Maryland, 1878), I, 207 & 205; Tanquerey, *Synopsis Theologiae Dogmaticae,* III, 496-497.

himself, so the letter states, could not carry or minister the last Sacrament, since he was ill. From this text it may be concluded that the priest ordinarily would have ministered the Viaticum himself.[57]

The thirty-second canon of the Council of Elvira (ca. 305) legislated as follows:

> "Apud presbyterum si quis gravi lapsu in ruinam mortis inciderit, placuit agere poenitentiam non debere, sed potius apud episcopum: cogente tamen infirmitate, necesse est presbyterum communionem praestare debere, et diaconum, si ei jusserit sacerdos."(1)

Another edition makes the canon read thus:

> "Si quis gravi lapsu in ruinam mortis inciderit, placuit agere poenitentiam non debere sine episcopi consultu, sed potius apud episcopum agat, cogente tamen infirmitate. Non est presbyterorum aut diaconorum communionem talibus praestare debere, nisi eis jusserit episcopus."(2)[58]

It must be noted that the meaning of this canon is disputed. The word *communio* was accepted in two senses: either as reconciliation of the penitent with the Church by sacramental and canonical absolution, or as the reception of the Holy Eucharist. Hefele (1809-1893) claimed that the title of this thirty-second canon should have read: De presbyteris ut excommunicatis in necessitate communionem dent. According to Hefele the canon legislated that only a bishop, not a priest, could reconcile (absolve) the penitent. During the illness of an excommunicate the priest or the deacon with the bishop's permission could give Communion to the absolved excommunicate.[59]

Frank (1827-1894) distinguished between sacramental and canonical absolution. He concluded that the canon permitted a deacon and *a fortiori* the priest, with the bishop's order, to confer

[57] Eusebius, *Ecclesiastical History,* Lib. VI, c. 44—*MPG,* XX, 630.

[58] (1) Mansi, II, 7; Hefele and Leclerq, *Histoire des Conciles* (10 vols. in 19, Paris, 1907-1938), I, pars I, 238 (hereafter cited as Hefele); (2) Hefele, I, pars I, 238.

[59] Cf. Hefele, I, pars I, 238.

on a sinner when already sacramentally absolved by the bishop the canonical absolution at the same time that he administered the Holy Eucharist.[60] Laurain held the same opinion.[61]

Morin (1591-1659) interpreted this enactment as granting the deacons the power of granting sacramental absolution with the bishop's permission. *A fortiori* the priest could likewise give sacramental absolution.[62]

Chardon (1595-1651) and Martène (1654-1739) cited this canon of the Council as proof that deacons were authorized in the early centuries to hear confessions in case of urgent necessity. Again the inference must be made that if the deacons were permitted, so much the more were the priests.[63]

The Council of Carthage which was held in the year 398 mentioned the *sacerdos* as the minister of penance and Communion for those who in sickness were thought to be near death. It must be noted that during these early centuries the word *sacerdos* signified the bishop as well as the priest. It was not until about the middle of the fifth century that this word became more restrictive in its meaning, especially when employed with reference to the penitential discipline. The relevant conciliar canon was later included by Gratian in his *Decretum*.[64]

The I Council of Braga (in Portugal) in 561 legislated that Viaticum and penance should be given *in exitu mortis* only when the bishop had considered and approved such an act. The *Glossa*

---

[60] *Die Bussdisciplin in der Kirche von den Apostelzeiten bis zum siebenten Jahrhundert* (Mainz, 1867), pp. 243-257.

[61] Cf. *De l'Intervention des Laïques, des Diacres et des Abbesses dans l'Administration de la Pénitence,* pp. 243-257.

[62] Cf. *Commentarius Historicus de Disciplina in Administratione Sacramenti Poenitentiae* (Antverpiae, 1682), Lib. II, c. 3, p. 158.

[63] Chardon, *Histoire des Sacrements*—Migne, *Theologiae Cursus Completus* (28 vols., Parisiis, 1839-1845), XX, 416 (hereafter cited as *MTC*); Martène, *De Antiquis Ecclesiae Ritibus,* Lib. I, pars. II, cap. 6, art. 6—I, 37.

[64] Can. 76: "Is qui poenitentiam in infirmitate petit, si casu, dum ad eum sacerdos invitatus venit, oppressus infirmitate obmutuerit vel in frenesim conversus fuerit, dent testimonium qui eum audierunt, et accipiat poenitentiam, et, si continuo creditur moriturus, reconcilietur per manus impositionem, et infundatur ori eius eucharistia."—c. 8, C. XXVI, q. 6; Bruns, I, 148; Mansi, III, 957.

Ordinaria in commenting on this text referred the law also to the giving of Holy Communion.[65]

Hugo Ménard (1585-1644), in his commentary on the Gregorian Sacramentary, pointed out that the sacramentary listed the priest as the minister of extreme unction and of Holy Viaticum.[66]

Of the thirty ordos contained in Marténe, nineteen of them explicitly mention Viaticum as having been administered along with extreme unction. And in all instances the priest was mentioned as the minister of both sacraments.[67]

The following legislation of the Middle Ages showed that the priest more than anyone else administered Viaticum. The *Fourth Statute* of St. Boniface promulgated in the Council of Lessines in 743 urged the priests not to journey without the holy Chrism, the blessed oil, and the sanctifying Eucharist. The statute urged them to be prepared for any emergency.[68]

In England, St. Egbert, Archbishop of York (735-766), formulated a statute in 748 which definitely stated that priests were ministers of Viaticum.[69]

Theodulf, Bishop of Orleans (798-818), in a capitulary to the priests of his diocese also mentioned priests as the ministers of Viaticum.[70]

---

[65] Can. 14: "Si quis de corpore exiens novissimum et necessarium communionis viaticum expetit, non ei denegetur. Quod si, in desperatione positus, post acceptam communionem iterum sanus fuerit factus, tantum oratione particeps sit, sacramentum vero non accipiat, donec institutum poenitentiae impleat tempus. Qui ergo in exitu mortis sunt et desiderant accipere sacramentum, cum consideratione et probatione episcopi accipere debent."—c. 6, C. XXVI, q. 6; Bruns, II, 58; *Glossa Ordinaria,* ad c. 6, C. XXVI, q. 6, s.v. *Si quis* and *impleat.*

[66] *Notae in S. Gregorii Librum Sacramentorum, Auctore D. Hugone Menardo, Monacho Benedictino—MPL,* LXXVIII, 522-533.

[67] Marténe, *De Antiquis Ecclesiae Ritibus,* Vol. I, pars II, 116-257.

[68] *S. Bonifatii Statuta,* c. 4.—*MPL,* LXXXIX, 822; Mansi, XII, 384 V.

[69] *Excerptiones S. Egberti (Eboracensis Archiepiscopi), Jus Sacerdotale XX*: "Ut cuncti sacerdotes omnibus illis confitentibus eorum crimina dignam poenitentiam cum summa vigilantia ipsis indicent, et omnibus infirmis ante exitum vitae viaticum et communionem corporis Christi misericorditer tribuant."—*MPL,* LXXXIX, 382; Mansi, XII, 415.

[70] *Theodulfi Capitulare ad Presbyteros Parochiae Suae (798)*:

"Admonendi etiam sunt sacerdotes de unctione infirmorum et poenitentia et viatico, ne aliquis sine viatico moriatur. . . . Tunc sacerdos det ei pacem et communicet eum."—*MPL,* CV, 220; Mansi, XIII, 996.

The Council of Aachen (836) likewise alluded to the sacerdotal ministry of Holy Viaticum.[71]

Prudentius, Bishop of Troyes (843-861), recording the life and death of the saintly virgin Maura, mentioned that he ministered Holy Eucharist to her at death.[72] Prudentius was the minister in this particular case rather than a priest, since he probably considered it a high honor and privilege to assist such a holy person at her death.

The Council of Mainz (847) legislated that the sick should be refreshed with the communion of Viaticum *per presbyteros.*[73] Likewise the Council of Pavia (850) in its eighth canon ordered that confession, extreme unction, and the Holy Eucharist be ministered by the priest of the place, or by neighboring priests, or by a bishop.[74]

The practice, however, of the laypeople's carrying and administering Viaticum continued long after the first centuries. In fact, this practice became an abuse to such an extent that especially in the ninth and tenth centuries, and even later, legislation had to be enacted to stop this practice.

In 650 the Council of Rouen prohibited priests from allowing laymen or laywomen to carry the Sacred Body of our Lord to the sick. Any violation of this legislation exposed the offender to the penalty of degradation. This canon was incorporated into the *Decree* of Gratian.[75]

Pope St. Leo IV (847-855) in a homily to the priests stated

---

[71] *Concilium Aquisgranense II (836), Ludovici Pii Aug. Jussu et Evocatione,* cap. 2, c. 5: "Denique, si finem urgentem perspexerit, commendet animam christianam Domino Deo suo more sacerdotali cum acceptione sacrae communionis."—*MGH,* Legum Sectio III, *Concilia,* tom. II, pars II, 711-712; Hardouin, IV, 1397.

[72] *Sermo de Vita et Morte B. V. Maurae—MPL,* CXV, 1574.

[73] C. 26—Hardouin, V, 13; Mansi, XIV, 932-933.

[74] Hardouin, V, 27; Mansi, XIV, 932-933.

[75] Cap. 2, can. 7: "Pervenit ad notitiam nostram quod quidam presbyteri in tantum parvipendunt divina mysteria ut laico aut foeminae Sacrum corpus Domini tradant ad deferendum infirmis. . . . Igitur interdicit per omnia Synodus ne talis temeraria praesumptio ulterius fiat; sed omnimodis presbyter per semetipsum infirmum communicet. Quod si aliter fecerit, gradus sui periculo subiacebit."—c. 29, D. II, *de cons.;* Bruns, II, 268.

that they should visit the sick, prepare them well, admonish and reconcile them, and communicate them *propria manu;* he forbade every priest to allow the laity, either men or women, to carry the Holy Eucharist to the sick.[76]

The Council of Anse (990), held near Lyons, permitted no one except priests to give Viaticum.[77]

Deacons, however, continued to administer Viaticum, at least in some places. This was shown by Chardon (1595-1651) in his reference to old statutes of the Carthusians.[78] The same practice was upheld by the Council of Westminster which was held in 1138.[79]

Bishop Etienne of Autun (1112-1139) wrote in the year 1136 that the deacon could take the place of the priest in certain duties. Among the duties enumerated was the administration of Holy Communion.[80] The Council of York (1195) legislated that the deacon could give Holy Communion only in the greatest necessity.[81]

Chardon, in speaking of the deacon's ministry of Viaticum, referred to William Beaumont, Bishop of Angers, as enacting in 1240 a synodal statute which forbade his priests to send a deacon with the Eucharist to the sick. The sole exception was urgent necessity.[82]

The Synod of Nimes (1284) made allowance for but two cases in which the deacon could minister Holy Communion: the case of

---

[76] *Homilia 947*—Mansi, XIV, 891; Jaffé, n. 2659; *MPL,* XCVI, 1375 sq.

[77] Can. 1: "Ac vetaverunt a nullo homine Corpus et Sanguinem praestare ad infirmum nisi sacerdotis solius."—Mansi, XIX, 101.

[78] *Histoire des Sacrements,* c. 5, art. 2—*MTC,* XX, 280.

[79] Can. 2: "Sancimus etiam ut ultra octo dies corpus Christi non reservetur; neque ad infirmos, nisi per sacerdotem, aut per diaconum, aut necessitate instante, per quemlibet cum summa reverentia deferatur."—Wilkins, *Concilia Magnae Brittaniae et Hiberniae a Synodo Verolamiensi A. D. 446 ad Londonensem A. D. 1717* (4 vols., London, 1737), I, 415.

[80] *De Sacramento Altaris,* c. 12: "In quibusdam habent [diaconi] vicem sacerdotis, ut in ministerio baptizandi, communicandi, delicta confitentium misericorditer suscipiendi."—*MPL,* CLXX, 1279.

[81] Can. 6: "Decrevimus etiam ut non nisi summa et gravi necessitate diaconus baptizet vel corpus Christi cuiquam eroget vel poenitentiam confitenti imponat. . . ."—Mansi, XXII, 653.

[82] *Histoire des Sacrements,* cap. 5, art. 2—*MTC,* XX, 280.

the absence of a priest, and the case of urgent necessity. In the latter case the deacon did not need the permission of the priest.[83]

Thus, from the legislation of the provincial councils and diocesan synods as here reviewed, it appears that the deacon functioned as the extraordinary minister of Viaticum, at least in England and in France, during the latter period of the Middle Ages.

Section 2. From the Decree of Gratian to the Council of Trent

From the *Decree* of Gratian it is plain that the law constituted and recognized the priest as the ordinary minister of Viaticum.[84] But from c. 18, D. XCIII, it is equally evident that the deacon was acknowledged as the extraordinary minister of Viaticum, i.e., of Communion in a case of urgent necessity. Recognition of this status of the deacon is also manifest in the *Glossa Ordinaria,* for in addition it pointed even to the faithful among the laity as extraordinary ministers in cases of urgent necessity.[85]

Gratian's collection moreover contained canons which restricted the monk's right in the ministry of Viaticum. Although Viaticum does not receive explicit mention in these canons, yet parochial duties in general could not be performed by the monks except in cases of urgent necessity, unless they had the bishop's permission and the abbot's consent, and unless it was by the free choice of the people that their services were desired.[86]

---

[83] Hardouin, VII, 914.

[84] Council of Worms (809), can. 16: "Presbiter eucharistiam semper habeat paratam, ut quando quis infirmatus fuerit, statim eum communicet, ne sine communione moriatur."—c. 93, D. II, *de cons.*

IV Council of Carthage (398), can. 38: "Praesente presbitero diaconus Eucharistiam corporis Christi populo, si necessitas cogat, iussus eroget."—c. 18, D. XCIII; Bruns, II, 145.

Council of Rouen (650), can. 2—c. 29, D. II, *de cons.;* Bruns, II, 268.

IV Council of Carthage (398), can. 76: "Is qui poenitentiam in infirmitate petit, si casu dum ad eum sacerdos invitatus venit, oppressus infirmitate obmutuerit vel in frenesim conversus fuerit, dent testimonium qui eum audierunt, et accipiat poenitentiam, et si creditur moriturus, reconcilietur per manus impositionem, et infundatur ori eius eucharistia."—c. 8, C. XXVI, q. 6; Bruns, I, 148.

[85] *Glossa Ordinaria* ad c. 29, D. II, *de cons.,* s. v. *Per semetipsum.*

[86] Cf. cc. 1-19, and 41, C. XVI, q. 1; cf. *infra,* pp. 28-29.

Pope Clement V (1305-1314) excommunicated the religious with an *ipso facto* incurred penalty reserved to the Holy See, if without permission they presumed to minister to clerics or to the laity the sacraments of extreme unction and the Eucharist, or if without permission they presumed to assist at the solemnization of marriages. But the same legislation granted the right to the monks to minister the sacraments to their domestics, to paupers, and also to guests residing at their monasteries.[87]

Leo X (1513-1521) decreed in 1516 that the Mendicants and the other Orders should not administer the sacraments of extreme unction and the Eucharist to the sick or to others to whom the proper priest had denied the reception of these two sacraments. The *proprius sacerdos* was accorded the prior right in the administration of these sacraments.[88]

ARTICLE 3. THE MINISTER OF EXTREME UNCTION

"Is any man sick among you? Let him bring in the priests of the Church, and let them pray over him, anointing him with oil in the name of the Lord: and the prayer of faith shall save the sick man; and the Lord shall raise him up; and if he be in sins, they shall be forgiven him."[89]

The clause, "Let him bring in the priests of the Church," was rendered in the original Greek text: "προσκαλεσάσθω τους πρεσβυτέρους τῆς εκκλησίας." What is the meaning of the term πρεσβύτεροι? In classical Greek the term referred to the elders or the *provecti aetate*. In the New Testament two general meanings are attached to the word elders: they were the bishops and priests, or they were the laymen in charge of a community. Thus in the *Acts of the Apostles* (XIV: 22), in the *Pastoral Epistles* (I Tim., V: 17 & 19; Tit., I: 5), and in St. Peter's *First Epistle* (V: 1) the term signified bishops and priests.

[87] C. I, *de privilegiis et excessibus privilegiatorum*, V, 7, in *Clem*, cf. *infra*, pp. 42-43.

[88] Const. *Dum intra*, 19 dec. 1516—*Bullarum Diplomatum et Privilegiorum Sanctorum Romanorum Pontificum Taurinensis Editio* (24 vols. et Appendix, Augustae Taurinorum-Neapoli, 1857-1872), V, 687 (hereafter cited as *Bull. Rom.*).

[89] St. James, V:14.

However, the term as used in the beginning of St. John's *Second* and *Third Epistles* had in all probability the meaning of an elderly person. In these texts it cannot be settled with certainty whether St. John was speaking of himself as an apostle, or as a very old man, or as the last of the apostles. A second instance of the same meaning is found in I Tim., V: 1 ff.: "An ancient man (πρεσβυτέρῳ) rebuke not, but entreat him as a father; young men, as brethren; etc." Here the impossibility of construing πρεσβύτερος in any other sense than *provectus aetate* is quite evident.[90]

Kilker (1901-1944) concluded the discussion thus:

> "The result must be consequently that the words τους πρεσβυτὲρους do not finally close the question that priests only are meant in the text of St. James. When used, however, with the determining clause τῆς εκκλησίας, the argument gains immense strength. It is hard to see how the complete phrase could signify any other personages than those who perform the sacred ministry, those who are called *priests* in the Church."[91]

Concerning this question the Council of Trent anathematized those who denied that only a priest could administer this last Sacrament.[92]

[90] Cf. Petavius, *Dogmata Theologica* (8 vols., Paris, 1866-1868), *Dissertationes Ecclesiasticae,* Lib. I, c. 2, n. 2—VIII, 410 sq.; Kurtscheid-Wilches, *Historia Iuris Canonici, Ad Usum Scholarium* (2 vols., Romae: Officium Libri Catholici, 1941-1943), *Historia Institutorum,* Vol. I (ab Ecclesiae Fundatione usque ad Gratianum), 15-20; Kilker, *Extreme Unction,* The Catholic University of America Canon Law Studies, n. 32 (Washington, D. C.: The Catholic University of America, 1926), pp. 11-12.

[91] Kilker, *Extreme Unction,* pp. 11-12; Cf. Corluy, *Specilegium Dogmatico-Biblicum* (3 vols., Gandavi, 1884), III, 453-454; Curci, *Il Nuovo Testamento* (3 vols., Romae, 1880), III, 479; *Lexicon Biblicum* (3 vols., ed. M. Hagen, Paris, 1911), in *Cursus Scripturae Sacrae* (auctoribus R. Cornely, J. Knabenbauer, F. Hummelauer), III, 678-679; Tanquerey, *Synopsis Theologiae Dogmaticae,* III, 699; J. Kern, *De Sacramento Extremae Unctionis Tractatus Dogmaticus* (Ratisbonae, 1907), pp. 241 sqq.; André-Wagner, *Dictionnaire du Droit Canonique* (5. ed., 4 vols., Paris, 1901), IV, 227.

[92] Sess. XIV, *De Extrema Unctione,* can. 4: "Si quis dixerit presbyteros Ecclesiae, quos S. Iacobus adducendos esse ad infirmum ungendum hortatur, non esse sacerdotes ab episcopo ordinatos, sed aetate seniores in quavis communitate; ob idque proprium Extremae Unctionis ministrum non esse solum sacerdotem, A. S."—Denzinger, *Enchiridion,* n. 929.

Section 1. From the First Centuries to the Decree of Gratian

An early evidence that both bishops and priests administered this sacrament is had in a letter written by Pope Innocent I (401-417) to Decentius, Bishop of Gubbio, in the year 416. From this epistle, which speaks of extreme unction, it may be concluded that the bishop certainly had the power to anoint, since what was permitted to the priest was *a fortiori* permitted to the bishop. The text stated that, since bishops were occupied with other tasks, the priests without doubt were permitted to minister the sacrament. This text is contained in Gratian's collection.[93]

Kallinikos in a writing on the life of his teacher St. Hypatius (ca. 366-446) gave evidence that the priest ministered this last sacrament.[94]

Origen (ca. 185-254) (1) and St. John Chrysostom (347-407) (2) in commenting on the Jacobean text pointed to the *"sacerdos"* as the minister of the last unction.[95]

St. Ambrose (340-397) in his work *De Poenitentia* gave evidence that the priest, designated specifically in the text with the word *presbyter,* was the minister of the last sacrament. The bishop, on the other hand, was the minister of the imposition of hands or of confirmation.[96]

Among the Armenians Patriarch John Mandakuni (ca. 480) exhorted his subjects to follow the command of St. James, to seek

---

[93] "Ceterum illud superfluum videmus adiectum, ut de episcopo ambigatur, quod presbyteris licere non dubium est. Nam idcirco de presbyteris dictum est, quia episcopi occupationibus aliis impediti ad omnes languidos ire non possunt."—c. 3, D. XCV; Jaffé, n. 311; *Fontes,* n. 19.

[94] "Si vero necessitas suaderet, infirmum oleo inungi debere monebat abbatem, qui presbyter erat, et curabat ab ipso perfici unctionem."—Cf. *Acta Sanctorum* (editio novissima curante Ioanne Carnandet, Parisiis et Romae, 1863-1870), June 17, IV, 251.

[95] (1) *Homilia II in Leviticum—MPG,* XII, 418 B; (2) *De Sacerdotio,* Lib. III, sect. 6—*MPG,* XLVIII, 644.

[96] C. 8: "Ceterum videtur hic signari ea benedictio, qua aegri a presbyteris inunguntur, precibusque Deo opt. Max. commendantur, ex praecepto Jacobi Ap. quem nos extremam unctionem appellamus. Nam praeterquam, quod huius sacramenti effectus etiam est aegri sanitas, de impositione manuum episcopi, seu confirmatione iam observavimus nihil curasse Novatianos."—*MPL,* XVI, 477.

the gift of grace from the priests, i.e., the anointing accompanied with a prayer. The patriarch made this exhortation so as to turn the sick away from the use of magical remedies, which practice was prevalent at that time among them.[97]

From these testimonies it may be concluded that during the early centuries both the bishop and the priest ministered the sacrament of extreme unction.

In the sixth century Cassiodorus (ca. 490-ca. 583), by the use of the term *presbyterum* in his text, seemed to give support to the custom of extreme unction being administered by the priest.[98]

Mention must be made at this point that there does not appear any evidence, even in the early centuries, to show that the rite of unction was administered solely as an episcopal function. Although historical documents speak of anointings administered by the bishops, nevertheless priests were not excluded from its ministry. For example, Charlemagne (+ 814) was anointed by a bishop; so, too, was St. Adelhard (+ 827), monk and abbot of Corbie, and one of Charlemagne's chief advisers. St. Mathilda (+ 968), mother of Emperor Otto I (936-973), received extreme unction from Archbishop Willelmus; Ferdinand III (1199-1252), ruler over Castile from 1217, and over Leon from 1230, was attended by a bishop.[99] In instances when the person was of royal rank, or when his sanctity was well recognized, it appeared more fitting and appropriate that the anointing be performed by a higher ranked member of the hierarchy.

Ancient rituals declared that if a bishop was present the rite of unction was his privilege.[100]

Durantis (1237-1296) spoke of the impropriety of a priest anointing someone who already had been anointed by a bishop.[101]

---

[97] Cf. Tanquerey, *Synopsis Theologiae Dogmaticae,* III, 681.

[98] *M. Aurelii Cassiodori Complexiones in Epp. Apostolorum*: "Nam si quis alterius praegravatur injuria vel corporis imbecillitate quassatur, presbyterum dicit adhibendum, qui oratione fidei et olei sancti perunctione concessa, salvet eum qui videtur afflictus. . . ."—*MPL,* LXX, 1380.

[99] Catalanus, *Rituale Romanum Benedicti Papae XII Jussu Editum* (2 vols., Patavii, 1760), I, 323.

[100] Martène, *De Antiquis Ecclesiae Ritibus Libri Quattuor,* Lib. I, c. 7, a. 4 (Ordo XII).

[101] *Rationale Divinorum Officiorum* (Neapoli, 1859), Lib. I, c. 8, n. 25.

However, during the Middle Ages particular councils and statutes throughout Western Europe legislated that priests were to minister this last sacrament. The following vindicated the right of ministry to them:

St. Sonnatius, Archbishop of Rheims (600-631), legislated even to the extent of making the pastor the proper minister. There is doubt, however, concerning the word *pastor* as used in this text. During the time of Sonnatius this term was not used, but rather the terms *presbyter* and *sacerdos*. Hence this word, it seems, was inserted into the text by a later writer.[102]

The fourth statute promulgated by St. Boniface in the Council of Lessines in 743 urged the priest not to journey anywhere without the Holy Chrism, the blessed oil, and the sanctifying Eucharist. It continued to urge the priests to be prepared for duty at all times under all circumstances.[103]

Egbert, Archbishop of York (748), Theodulf, Bishop of Orleans, in a capitulary to the priests (798), the Council of Chalon-sur-Saône (813), Jonas, Bishop of Orleans (829), Amolo, Bishop of Lyons (841), the Council of Mainz under Archbishop Rabanus (847), and the Council of Pavia (850), all specified the priest as the minister not only of extreme unction, but in many cases also of the sacrament of penance for penitents in danger of death, and of Holy Viaticum.[104]

In the early centuries Pope Innocent I (401-417) and other early writers seemed to give evidence in their writing to the ministry of sacred oil by lay people. According to these writings it

---

[102] *S. Sonatii Rhemensis Episcopi Statuta,* cap. 15: "Extrema unctio deferatur laboranti et petenti, eumque *pastor* in propria saepius invisat, et pie visitet, eum ad futuram gloriam animando, et debite praeparando."—Mansi, X, 596; *MPL,* LXXX, 444.

[103] *S. Bonifatii Statuta,* c. 4—*MPL,* LXXXIX, 822; Mansi, XII, 384 V.

[104] *Excerptiones S. Egberti (Eboracensis Archiepiscopi),* Iura XX, XXI, XXII—*MPL,* LXXXIX, 382; Mansi, XII, 415; *Theodulfi Capitulares ad Presbyteros Parochiae Suae*—*MPL,* CV, 220; Mansi, XIII, 996; *Concilium Cabilonense* II (813), c. 48—Mansi, XIV, 104; Hardouin, IV, 1040; *Institutio Laicalis,* Lib. III, c. 12—*MPL,* CV, 260-261; *Epistola Prima ad Theobaldum*-*MPL,* CXVI, 82; *Concilium Moguntinum* (847), c. 26—Hardouin, V, 13; Mansi, XIV, 910; *Synodus Regeaticina* (850), c. 8—Hardouin, V, 27; Mansi, XIV, 932-933.

seems to have been an accepted custom for lay people to anoint not only others but also themselves.[105]

Concerning the text of Pope Innocent I Kilker stated:

> "Divorced from its context, this question seems rather convincing; but a review of the entire epistle will furnish the correct impression that the doubt decided by Innocent was not whether or not the ministration of this Sacrament might be extended to the laity, but rather whether it was an exclusively episcopal function. Decentius questioned even the validity of priestly unction, and hence there was no query at all about the capability of laymen in the matter."[106]

Hurter (1832-1914) suggested that the word *"uti"* was used in a passive sense, i.e., *uti licet, sed ministerio sacerdotum.*[107]

Some authors maintained that an official and a private use of the oil was distinguished by the Pope, and that consequently the private unction was merely a sacramental, while the official unction

---

[105] Innocentius I, Ep. *"Si instituta ecclesiastica,"* 19 mart. 416: "Non est dubium quod de fidelibus aegrotantibus accipi vel intelligi debere, qui sancto oleo chrismatis perungi possunt; quo ab episcopo confecto, non solum sacerdotibus sed omnibus uti Christianis licet in sua aut suorum necessitate inungendo."—*Fontes,* n. 19; S. Eligius, Episcopus Naviomensis (640-659), *De Rectitudine Catholicae Conversationis,* n. 5:—"Qui aegrotat in sola misericordia Dei confidat, et Eucharistiam corporis et sanguinis Christi cum fide et devotione accipiat, oleumque benedictum fideliter ab Ecclesia petat, unde *corpus suum* in nomine Christi *ungat* et secundum Apostolum oratio fidei salvabit infirmum et alleviabit eum Dominus. . . ."—*MPL,* XL, 1178. St. Caesarius Arelatensis (ca. 502-ca. 542), *Sermo CCLXV in appl. Serm. S. Augustini*: "Quoties aliqua infirmitas supervenerit, corpus et sanguinem Christi ille qui aegrotat accipiat; et inde *corpusculum suum ungat* ut illud, quod scriptum est, impletur in eo: 'Infirmatur aliquis, inducat presbyteros et orent super eum, ungentes eum oleo' . . . Videte fratres, quia qui in infirmitate ad Ecclesiam cucurrerit, et corporis sanitatem recipere et peccatorum indulgentiam merebitur obtinere."—*MPL,* XXXIX, 2238. (The important words in these texts were italicized by the writer.)

[106] Kilker, *Extreme Unction,* p. 82.

[107] Cf. *Theologiae Dogmaticae Compendium* (12. ed., 3 vols., Oentiponte, 1909), III, 478, footnote I.

was a sacrament, whose administration was reserved to the bishops and the priests.[108]

Schell (1850-1906) suggested another explanation: The Pope's decision was probably to be understood as applying to a sort of unction by desire in a case of necessity (an analogue of lay confession), which desire manifested the patient's good will to do what was in his power.[109]

Regarding the text of St. Eligius it may be stated that the custom of the Greek language often allowed the use of the active form in a passive voice. Kilker pointed to the fact that many manuscripts read "*ungatur*" instead of "*ungat.*"[110]

Furthermore, St. Eligius was speaking of the anointment "*in nomine Christi*" and "*secundum Apostolum.*" Hence he referred to the unction performed as the Apostle had prescribed, i.e., by priests. Kilker also pointed out that the Greeks spoke of the subject in the active voice (ὁ ποιῶν, ὁ ποησας τὸ εὐχέλαιον), or in the middle voice (ὁ ἐπαλειψάμενος). All these considerations conspire to show that St. Eligius was speaking of the reception rather than of the administration of this sacrament.[111]

The same defense is given for the text of St. Caesarius of Arles.

Upon the examination of the early writings and rituals, one finds that either one priest or several priests validly and licitly administered the sacrament. Among those who spoke of the minister in the singular number were Cassiodorus and Kallinikos in relating the life of St. Hypatius (ca. 366-446). Practically all of the previously mentioned statutes and particular councils of the Middle Ages spoke of simply one minister.[112]

A large number of early rituals made provision for but one minister.[113]

---

[108] Pohle-Preuss, *The Sacraments* (3. revised edition, 4 vols., St. Louis, 1919-1920), IV, 14; Bord, *L'Extreme Onction* (Bruges, 1923), p. 102.

[109] Cf. *Katholische Dogmatik* (4 vols., Paderborn, 1889-1893), III, 623.

[110] Cf. *Extreme Unction*, p. 83.

[111] Cf. Kern, *De Sacramento Extremae Unctionis Tractatus Dogmaticus*, pp. 16-17.

[112] *Ep. S. Jacobi ad Dispersos*, n. 2—*MPL*, LXX, 1380; *Acta Sanctorum*, June 17, IV, 251; cf. *supra*, p. 25.

[113] Cf. Marténe, *De Antiquis Ecclesiae Ritibus Libri Quattuor*, Lib. I, cap. 7, art. 4 (Ordines XII, XXVIII, XXIX); *Notae in S. Gregorii Librum*

Marténe's collection of *ordines* which range from the third to the fifteenth century listed seven *ordines* from a total number of thirty as indicating a plurality of ministers.[114]

Section 2. From the Decree of Gratian to the Council of Trent

Gratian's *Decree* does not reveal much legislation on the sacrament itself or on its minister. His collection contains the above mentioned letter of Pope Innocent I to Bishop Decentius of Gubbio. With reference to it Gratian showed that the ministers of extreme unction were both the bishop and the priest.[115]

The rights of monks in parochial duties are found restricted to their exercise within the monasteries. According to Gratian's *Decree* monks could not perform parochial duties without the bishop's permission, the abbot's consent, and the desire of the people as motivated by their own free choice. Although extreme unction was not explicitly mentioned, yet its ministry was regarded as the fulfillment of a parochial duty, and precluded from the scope of activity which the monks could lawfully exercise outside their monasteries.[116]

Sacramentorum, auctore D. Hugone Ménardo, Monacho Benedictino—MPL, LXXVIII, 225 D; Cabrol-LeClerq, *Monumenta Ecclesiae Liturgica* (6 vols., Parisiis, 1900-1902), *Ordo ad Visitandum vel Perungendum Infirmum (Mozarabic Rite)*, V, 71.

[114] Cf. *De Antiquis Ecclesiae Ritibus Libri Quattuor,* Lib. I, cap. 7, art. 4 (Ordines IV, XI, XII, XIX, XXII, XXIV, XXX).

[115] Cf. c. 3, D. XCV: "Illud superfluum videmus adiectum, ut de episcopo ambigatur, quod presbyteris licere non dubium est. Nam idcirco de presbyteris dictum est, quia episcopi occupationibus aliis impediti ad omnes languidos ire non possunt. Ceterum, si episcopus aut potest, aut dignum ducit aliquem a se visitandum, et benedicere, et tangere crismate, sine cunctatione potest, cuius est ipsum crisma conficere."—Jaffé, n. 311.

[116] Cf. cc. 1-19, and 41, C. XVI, q. 1: *Dictum* p. c. 19: ". . . Monachi autem, et si dedicatione sui presbiteratus (sicut et ceteri sacerdotes) praedicandi, baptizandi, penitentiam dandi, peccata remittendi, beneficiis ecclesiasticis perfruendi rite potestatem accipiant, ut amplius et perfectius agant ea, quae sacerdotalis offitii esse sanctorum Patrum constitutionibus conprobantur: tamen executionem suae potestatis non habent, nisi a populo fuerint electi, et ab episcopo cum consensu abbatis ordinati." Dictum p. c. 25: "His omnibus auctoritatibus perspicue monstratur, monachos posse penitentiam dare, baptizare, et cetera sacerdotalia officia licite administrare. Quod vero populi electione, episcoporum institutione, et abbatis consensu potestatem suam exequi valeant, Ieronimi, Gelasii et Gregorii auctoritate probatur."

Pope Clement V (1305-1314) enacted an excommunication, *ipso facto* to be incurred as a penalty reserved to the Holy See, by those monks who presumed without the permission of the parochial priest to minister to clerics or to the laity the sacraments of extreme unction and of the Eucharist, or to assist at the solemnization of marriages. The same legislation, however, acknowledged to monks the right to minister the sacraments to their domestics, to paupers, and to those who resided as guests at the monastery.[117]

The *Glossa Ordinaria* in commenting on this text stated that the sacraments of the Eucharist and of extreme unction should be received from the proper priest. In regard to the administration of the sacraments by the monks in their own monasteries, the same *Glossa* stated that the Pope could grant a general privilege to all, or the bishop also could grant a special concession to such as belonged to the monastery located within his diocese.[118]

The proper priest was defined by St. Raymond of Pennafort (ca. 1175-1275) as one having the ordinary pastoral care of his subjects. This *cura animarum* had to be shared with the priest by his bishop.[119]

The Decretals of Gregory IX (1227-1241) through incorporating the legislation of Alexander III (1159-1181) stated that even one priest could administer extreme unction: "Solus sacerdos potest sacramentum extremae unctionis infirmo conferre."[120]

Two centuries later Pope Eugene IV (1431-1447) similarly decreed that the minister of this sacrament is a priest.[121]

Finally, Pope Leo X (1513-1521) legislated that the Mendicants as also the priests of the other Orders were not to administer

---

[117] C. I, *de privilegiis et excessibus privilegiatorum,* V, 7, in Clem.

[118] Cf. *Glossa Ordinaria*: *In casu* s. c. 1, *de privilegiis et excessibus privilegiatorum,* V, 7, in Clem.: "Colligo aliqua notabilia, primo quod quilibet tenetur recipere sacramenta Eucharistiae et extremae Unctionis, et alia sacramenta a suo proprio sacerdote. . . ." Cf. *Glossa Ordinaria* s. v. *Apostolica* ad c. I, *de privilegiis et excessibus privilegiatorum,* V, 7, in Clem.

[119] Cf. *Summa,* Lib. III, tit. 34, *De Poenitentiis et Remissionibus,* sect. 4, *De Confessione,* p. 424.

[120] C. 14, X, *de verborum significatione,* V, 40; Jaffé, n. 12184.

[121] Const. *Exultate Deo,* 22 nov. 1439—*Bull. Rom.* V, 50.

the sacraments of extreme unction and the Eucharist to an ill person to whom his pastor as the proper priest had denied the reception of these two sacraments. The *proprius sacerdos* possessed the prior right for their administration.[122]

---

[122] Const. *Dum intra,* 19 dec. 1516—*Bull. Rom.* V, 687.

CHAPTER II

THE MINISTER OF THE LAST SACRAMENTS SINCE THE COUNCIL OF TRENT (1545-1563)

ARTICLE 1. THE MINISTER OF LAST CONFESSION

The Council of Trent, convened by Pope Paul III (1534-1549) to effect a much needed reform throughout the Church, speaking of sacramental confession in general legislated that the bishops and priests alone were its ministers. Concerning the last confession the Council legislated that any person who was in immediate danger of death could be absolved both validly and licitly from any sin or censure by any validly ordained priest.[1]

The Catechism of the Council of Trent for Parish Priests, issued by order of Pope Pius V (1566-1572), taught that the minister of penance in cases of imminent danger of death was any priest. It was lawful for any priest, not only to remit all kinds of sins, whatever faculties they might otherwise require, but also to absolve from excommunication.[2]

However, if the danger of death which existed was not imminent, then it seemed that the stricken persons had to confess to those confessors to whom they confessed under ordinary circumstances. Thus, an analysis is made of the valid and licit ordinary confessors of various classes of the faithful.

Section 1. The Pastor's Right to the Hearing of the Confessions of His Parishioners and of All Others Subject to His Jurisdiction

Schmalzgrueber (1663-1735) stated that the penitential forum to which the parishioners and all others who came under his juris-

[1] Sess. VII, *de sacramentis in genere*, can. 10; Sess. XIV, *de sanctissimo poenitentiae sacramento*, can. 6-7; Sess. XXIII, *de sacramento ordinis*, can. 1.

[2] Callan and McHugh, *Catechism of the Council of Trent for Parish Priests* (Seventh Printing, New York: Wagner, 1943), Part II, *Penance*, p. 291.

diction were subject was such that absolution when granted by any other priest than the pastor was invalid, since other priests lacked the necessary jurisdiction. Only with the consent of the pastor could another priest hear the confessions of the pastor's subjects.[3] Accordingly, when any priest was called by a parishioner to hear his last confession outside of a case of urgent necessity occasioned by an imminent danger of death, then such a priest was precluded from accepting the call if he lacked the proper pastor's authorization. The parishioner who was not in imminent danger of death was obliged to confess to his pastor or to a priest to whom the pastor had given his consent for the hearing of the particular confession.

However, Van Espen (1646-1728) at the beginning of the eighteenth century stated that in his time the faithful were free to choose any confessor. But the faithful were obliged to confess once a year during Lent or during the Paschal time to their respective pastors. Yet even this annual confession could be heard by another priest if he had at least the tacit or presumed permission of the pastor.[4] Thus it seems that at the beginning of the eighteenth century the pastor's claim to exclusive jurisdiction in respect to the hearing of confessions under ordinary circumstances was no longer sustained in general practice. Furthermore, the commentators did not even so much as imply that the hearing of a parishioner's last confession was the pastor's exclusive right, as was the administration of extreme unction and Holy Viaticum.

All the commentators noted also the privilege which had been granted by the various Pontiffs to practically all the regulars. This privilege granted them the right, even apart from seeking the pastor's permission, to hear the confessions of all the faithful who approached them, and also of the sick who called them to their homes. The Council of Trent, however, insisted that the bishop's approbation of each religious confessor was required before he could share this privilege.[5]

---

[3] *Ius Ecclesiasticum Universum* (5 vols. in 12, Romae, 1843-1845), Lib. III, tit. 29, n. 2.

[4] *Compendium Iuris Ecclesiastici* (2 vols., Bassani, 1784), I, tit. VI, cap. 6, n. 58.

[5] "Nullum etiam Regularem posse confessiones saecularium, etiam sacerdotum, audire, nec ad id idoneum reputari, nisi aut parochiale beneficium,

Pirhing (1606-1679) stated that after hearing the confession of a sick person the religious was obliged to inform the proper pastor of that fact.[6]

In his commentary Maschat (1692-1747) pointed to a decree which ordered every confessor, whether secular or regular, under penalty of *ipso facto* incurring a suspension from the hearing of confession, to inform the pastor of the sick person as well as the attending physician of the fact that he had heard the confession of the stricken person. It must be noted, however, that this particular decree could not be traced in any other work. It appears to be found only in Maschat's commentary.[7]

In regard to last confession outside the imminent danger of death, the parishioners as well as all others subject to the pastor's jurisdiction could confess either to the pastor or to any other priest, whether secular or regular, provided, of course, that this priest had the proper approbation for the hearing of confessions.

Section 2. Ministers of Confession of the Religious

A. For Men Religious of Solemn or Simple Vows

The ordinary confessor until the Council of Trent seemed to be the religious superior or his delegate.[8] Under ordinary circumstances, then, the last confession of a regular was heard by the superior or his delegate.

A few privileges were granted to individual Orders, namely, of choosing on two occasions, i.e., once during life and also at the time of death, a confessor who thereby received faculties to

---

aut ab episcopis per examen, si illis videbitur esse necessarium, aut alias idoneus iudicetur, et approbationem, quae gratis detur, obtineat; privilegiis et consuetudine quacumque, etiam immemorabili, non obstantibus."—Sess. XXIII, *de ref.*, c. 15.

[6] *Ius Canonicum Nova Methodo Explicatum* (5 vols., Dilingae, 1674-1678), Lib. I, tit. 31, n. 145; S. C. Ep. et Reg., 2 iul. 1587; *Senogallien.*, 22 ian. 1616. (These decrees are mentioned in Van Espen's work, but do not seem to be traceable in other works or in any collection of the sources.)

[7] *Institutiones Canonicae* (4 vols. in 2, Florentiae, 1854), Lib. V, tit. 38, n. 4; Urban VIII, "Sacra Congregatio Visitationis," 1625.

[8] McCormick, *Confessors of Religious*, pp. 15-19.

absolve from censures. As a rule these confessors were of the same Order and were chosen only with the permission of the superior.[9]

Some few Orders even received the privilege of choosing any confessor, whether regular or secular, whose faculties of absolution thereby extended to all cases of excommunication, interdict, and suspension, even if reserved to the bishop either by the law or by the bishop's own ordinance. Such confessors could absolve as often as necessary. Consequently all those who enjoyed this privilege could use such confessors for the last confession also.[10]

McCormick stated that all these privileges were exceptions to the general law of unity of the confessor and did in no way mitigate the general discipline. In fact, the reverse was very much in evidence, for many were forbidden to confess outside of their Order.[11]

Clement VIII (1592-1605) in his decree *Sanctissimus Dominus* excluded superiors from the office of confessor of their own religious, but he left the choice of two or more confessors for individual houses entirely in their hands.[12] This meant that the regulars had a choice of confessing in their last moments to any of two or more confessors, to the exclusion, however, of the superior, unless the danger of death was imminent.

In the course of time exceptions tending towards a relaxation of the law of the unity of confessor were made by different Pontiffs for various reasons. Benedict XIV (1740-1758) granted to the Capuchins who were outside of their monastery with the permission of their superior the right to confess lawfully in the absence of a priest of their own Order to any secular priest approved by his proper superiors. Under these same circumstances these regulars could make their last confession to the same priests.[13]

This same permission was granted by Pope Pius IX (1846-1878) to the Regulars of the Order of the Sacred Heart of Mary,

---

[9] Cf. McCormick, *Confessors of Religious,* p. 17.

[10] Cf. McCormick, *op. cit.,* p. 18.

[11] *Op. cit.,* pp. 18-19.

[12] 26 maii 1593—*Fontes,* n. 177.

[13] Const. *Quod communi,* 30 maii 1742—*Bull. Rom.,* I, 175.

who belonged to the suppressed apostolic college of the Blessed Virgin Mary in the Diocese of Guadalajara.[14]

In 1913 Pius X (1903-1914) granted the members of all religious Orders, congregations, and institutes full freedom to validly and licitly confess to all their sacerdotal confrères or to any secular or regular priest who enjoyed episcopal approbation. By this legislation the regulars could call any priest who had episcopal approbation to hear his last confession. This granted them freedom in the choice of a confessor, although the constitutions of religious institutes concerning the ordinary confessors and confession at definite times still had full force.[15]

McCormick in speaking of men religious of simple vows stated that the congregations of priests of simple vows were ruled by the same laws as regulars, but that other male religious of simple vows were not subject to the discipline of the unity of confessor. Therefore, male lay religious who were subject to the bishop could validly confess to any confessor who was approved by the bishop for hearing the confessions of the faithful. It was the mind of the Holy See that male lay religious, if subject to exempt religious superiors, be given the same facilities through the appointment of several confessors in one house.[16]

B. For Nuns and Sisters

Just as the regular superiors until the Council of Trent preserved the exclusive right of hearing the confessions of their male subjects either themselves or through their delegate, so they also observed the same practice in regard to the nuns subject to them. Hence the minister of the last confession was the regular superior or his delegate.[17]

---

[14] S. C. Ep. et Reg., 4 iul. 1862—*Collectanea in Usum Secretariae Sacrae Congregationis Episcoporum et Regularium*, cura A. Bizzarri, secretarii (Romae, 1885), p. 155 (hereafter cited as Bizzarri).

[15] 5 aug., *Acta Apostolicae Sedis, Commentarium Officiale* (Romae, 1909-1929; Civitate Vaticana, 1929-), V (1913), 431 (hereafter cited as *AAS*); cf. McCormick, *Confessors of Religious*, pp. 29-30.

[16] Cf. *Confessors of Religious*, p. 25.

[17] Cf. McCormick, *op. cit.*, p. 82.

It was with a view to giving more freedom of conscience to the nuns that the Council of Trent published its decree on the confessors of nuns on December 3, 1563. This law, which from its very wording applied only to nuns, granted them: 1) an ordinary confessor, whose duty it was to hear all the confessions of the nuns, and 2) an extraordinary confessor who was to go to the convent for the same purpose two or three times a year.[17a] Consequently, a nun who was stricken by an illness, for example, but was not in immediate danger of death, confessed either to the ordinary or the extraordinary confessor.

Benedict XIV granted the sick nuns permission to request of their respective superiors, whether the bishop or the regular prelate, the appointment of a particular confessor. Upon failure to honor their request the sick nuns could apply to the Cardinal Penitentiary.[18]

McCormick stated that the common law until the latter half of the eighteenth century did not explicitly treat of institutes of sisters or of women religious professed with simple vows, nor did the law impose upon them the law of the unity of confessor. They were subject in this matter to the will of the bishops. The latter, however, had the practice of appointing only one ordinary confessor. But McCormick pointed out that the Constitution *Pastoralis curae,* which granted the above mentioned privilege to nuns and moreover insisted on the appointment of two confessors for each convent of the nuns, applied also to congregations which had but one ordinary confessor.[19] In consequence of that ruling sisters received the right of having their last confessions heard by either the ordinary or the extraordinary confessor, or by any confessor whom the sisters requested, provided that he was properly approved by his legitimate superior. In cases of imminent danger of death any validly ordained priest could be summoned.

In 1890 the decree *Quemadmodum* was published. However, it did not change the previously existing discipline. It introduced

---

[17a] Sess. XXV, *de regularibus,* c. 10.

[18] Const. *Pastoralis curae,* 5 aug. 1748—*Fontes,* n. 388.

[19] Cf. *Confessors of Religious,* pp. 92-93.

greater uniformity and security in the matter of the confessors of women religious.[20]

ARTICLE 2. THE MINISTER OF HOLY VIATICUM AND EXTREME UNCTION

The Council of Trent did not specifically legislate on the ministry of Holy Viaticum. However, it did restate the doctrine that the priests were the consecrators and the ministers of Holy Communion.[21]

The Catechism of the Council of Trent also taught nothing specifically concerning the ministry of Holy Viaticum. It reiterated the doctrine of the Council on the minister of the Eucharist. The Catechism stated that only priests had powers to consecrate and administer this sacrament.[22]

Regarding the ministry of extreme unction the Fathers of the Council legislated that the proper ministers of this last sacrament were the priests of the Church. They decreed that by the name *priests* were to be understood not the elders of the people or such as ranked highest among them, but either the bishops themselves, or priests rightly ordained by the bishops with the imposition of the hands of the priesthood.[23]

The Catechism of the Council of Trent not only repeated the doctrine of the Council but it added that not to every priest has the administration of this sacrament been committed, but to the proper priest who has jurisdiction, or to some other priest authorized by the proper priest to discharge this office.[24]

---

[20] S. C. Ep. et Reg., decr. *Quemadmodum,* 17 dec. 1890—*Collectanea Sacrae Congregationis de Propaganda Fide* (2 vols., Romae, 1907), n. 1745; *Fontes,* n. 2017.

[21] Sess. XIII, *de Eucharistia,* c. 8; Sess. XXIII, *de sacramento ordinis,* can. 1.

[22] Callan and McHugh, *Catechism of the Council of Trent for Parish Priests,* Part II, *The Eucharist,* p. 253.

[23] Sess. XIV, *doctrina de sacramento extremae unctionis,* c. 3; Sess. XIV, *de sacramento extremae unctionis,* can. 4.

[24] Callan and McHugh, *op. cit.,* Part II, *Extreme Unction,* p. 314.

Section 1. The Valid Minister

Barbosa (1589-1649) pointed out that Holy Viaticum could be ministered validly not only by any priest, but also by a deacon.[25]

Barbosa also pointed out the fact that any priest could validly minister the sacrament of extreme unction, since the administration of this sacrament was intrinsically not an act of jurisdiction such as was the act of absolving from sins. Even an excommunicated or a suspended priest could validly minister the sacrament.[26]

Section 2. The Licit Minister

Before anyone could licitly administer these two sacraments, two general conditions had to be fulfilled: The minister had to possess jurisdiction over the stricken person, and it was, furthermore, necessary that he be not impeded in any way by the Church from the licit administration of these sacraments, as, for example, through suspension or excommunication.

If one did not have jurisdiction over the sick person, then for the licit administration he had to obtain the delegated faculty from the proper priest who possessed that jurisdiction. A priest who ministered the sacraments to the dying without the proper priest's permission or the bishop's, in fact without even the hope of a later approval from the same, not only ministered illicitly, but also sinned gravely.

In fact, religious who administered these two last sacraments without the special permission of the parish priest incurred *ipso facto* an excommunication reserved to the Holy See. However, this provision did not apply to the religious who had been granted permission by the Holy See to administer the sacraments to their domestics or to the poor residing in their religious houses.[27]

This enactment was supposedly legislated at the Council of

---

[25] Cf. *De Officio et Potestate Parochi Descriptio* (ed. U. Giraldi a S. Cajetano, Romae, 1774), Pars II, cap. 23, n. 3; Laymann (1574-1635), *Theologia Moralis* (2 vols., Patavii, 1783), Lib. V, tract. 8, cap. 6, n. 2.

[26] Cf. *op. cit.,* Pars II, cap. 22, n. 1.

[27] Barbosa, *De Officio et Potestate Parochi Descriptio,* Pars II, cap. 22, n. 2; Laymann, *Theologia Moralis,* Lib. V, tract. 8, cap. 6, n. 2.

Vienne (1311-1312), and was in effect even until the promulgation of the present Code.[28]

The only exceptions to the above stated general law were the cases of urgent necessity. When the stricken person was in such danger of death that there was not sufficient time to call for the proper minister, or if the latter could not or would not come, then any priest could licitly minister both extreme unction and Holy Viaticum, even an excommunicated priest. Under such circumstances even a deacon could licitly minister Holy Viaticum. A religious, too, although without any permission, could administer the sacraments without incurring the excommunication.[29]

In what follows there will be a treatment of those persons who were constituted as licit ministers, and of the limits within which the licit ministers could rightfully exercise their faculty for the administration of the two last sacraments.

A. The Parish Priest

By way of an introductory statement it should be noted that from the Council of Trent until the present Code great stress was placed on the obligations of the pastor toward his parishioners and vice versa. The Council of Trent commanded all bishops to assign clearly marked boundaries for parishes in such a manner that each parish be composed of people in a certain definite territory, to whom one pastor was appointed to care for their spiritual needs. The pastor was to enjoy exclusive jurisdiction over the people assigned to him, and from him alone could they licitly receive the sacraments.[30]

Speaking of the relationship between the pastor and his parishioners, Cardinal De Luca (1614-1683) stated that the right of the

[28] Cf. Schroeder, *Disciplinary Decrees of the General Councils, Text, Translation, and Commentary* (St. Louis: Herder, 1937), p. 434; cf. Pius IX, const. *Apostolicae Sedis,* 12 oct. 1869—*Fontes,* n. 552.

[29] Pirhing, *Ius Canonicum Nova Methodo Explicatum,* Lib. I, tit. 31, nn. 143 and 152.

[30] ". . . unicuique suum perpetuum peculiaremque parochum assignet, qui eas cognoscere valeat, et a quo solo licite sacramenta suscipiant. . . ." Sess. XXIV, *de ref.,* c. 13.

pastor, and conversely the corresponding obligation of his parishioners, consisted in the mutual necessity for the pastor to administer the sacraments to his own parishioners exclusively, and for the parishioners to receive them from him to the exclusion of the other ministers.[31]

As for the administration of the last sacraments, all commentators unanimously stated that the administration of Holy Viaticum and of extreme unction was an exclusive right of the pastor.[32]

The local pastor had both the right and the obligation of ministering the last sacraments to the following:

1. To his parishioners who were domiciled within the parish limits when illness overtook them.

2. To all others who, though they held domiciles elsewhere, were actually stricken while resident in the local pastor's parish. Under such circumstances the pastor of the parish where the person became sick administered the sacraments. This statement is based on the decisions of the Sacred Congregations as well as on the common practice of the past centuries, as related by the post-Tridentine writers. De Luca pointed out, however, that in view of his temporary and transitory abode in another parish, a sick person did not cease to be a parishioner of his respective pastor.[33]

---

[31] *Theatrum veritatis et iustitiae, seu decisivi discursus ad veritatem editi in forensibus controversiis canonicis et civilibus* (16 vols. in 4, Romae, 1706), *De Parocho,* disc. XXIII, n. 8 (hereafter cited as *Theatrum veritatis et iustitiae*).

[32] Cf. Barbosa, *De Officio et Potestate Parochi Descriptio,* Pars II, cap. 22, n. 2 and cap. 20, n. 2; Laymann, *Theologia Moralis,* Lib. V, tract. 8, cap. 6, n. 2 and Lib. V, tract. 4, cap. 7, n. 33; Pirhing, *Ius Canonicum Nova Methodo Explicatum,* Lib. I, tit. 31, nn. 143 and 152; Schmalzgrueber, *Ius Ecclesiasticum Universum,* Lib. III, tit. 29, n. 10; Van Espen, *Compendium Iuris Ecclesiastici,* I, tit. 8, cap. 3, n. 26 and tit. 4, cap. 5, n. 34; Maschat, *Institutiones Canonicae,* II, Lib. III, tit. 29, n. 3; Pehem (1741-1799), *Ius Ecclesiasticum Universum* (2 vols., Viennae, 1785), II, sect. 2, art. 1, nn. 385 and 409; Wernz (1842-1914), *Ius Decretalium* (2. ed., 6 vols., Romae et Prati, 1906-1913), II, pars II, tit. 39; Zitelli (+ 1887), *Apparatus Iuris Ecclesiastici* (Romae, 1888), Lib. II, art. 5, n. 374, and Lib. II, art. 3, n. 323.

[33] *Theatrum veritatis et iustitiae, De Parocho,* disc. XXIII, n. 9: "Non facit cessare iurisdictionem proprii parochi, neque illam inducit in eo, intra

To a query whether pilgrims, travelers, strangers, foreigners, rulers and their substitutes, officials and their agents, emissaries, military officers, soldiers, the incarcerated, and those who had been condemned to die were so subject to the cathedral churches that theirs was the right of administering the sacraments, or whether the right belonged to the parochial churches where they lived and died, the Sacred Congregation of the Council replied that the question should be decided in the light of a full examination of the local customs and agreements.[34]

3. To cathedral and collegiate canons if sickness befell them in their domiciles which were distinct from the canons' residence. If, however, they resided permanently in the proper residence of the canons, then the cathedral priest administered the sacraments.[35]

At times, however, an apostolic privilege or legitimate custom permitted a canon to receive the sacraments from the collegiate church instead of from the church of the domiciliary pastor.[36]

To ill minor clerics and priests. These received the last sacraments from the parish priest, and not from the cathedral priest, unless a centenary or an immemorial custom or an apostolic privilege warranted otherwise.[37]

Barbosa stated that if the pastor himself was taken ill, then

---

cuius parochiae limites huiusmodi accidentale seu causativum domicilium habeatur."

[34] S. C. C. in Savonen. *Iurium parochialium,* 12 nov., 13 dec. 1712, 17 iun. 1713—Pallottini, *Collectio omnium conclusionum et resolutionum quae in causis propositis apud Sacram Congregationem Cardinalium S. Concilii Tridenti Interpretum prodierunt ab eius institutione anno MDLXIV ad annum MDCCCLX* (18 vols., Romae, 1868-1895), s. v. *De Parocho,* XIV, n. 19 (hereafter cited as Pallottini).

[35] S. C. C., *Tiburtina,* 12 maii 1685—*Fontes,* n. 2886; S. C. C., *Tolentinaten.,* 11 sept. 1694—*Fontes,* n. 2944; S. C. C., *Novarien.,* 27 aug. 1695, ad 1—*Fontes,* n. 2950; S. C. C., *Narnien.,* 26 sept. 1699—*Fontes,* n. 2971; S. C. C. in *S. Miniatis Iurium parochialium,* 24 nov. 1621—Pallottini, s. v. *De Parocho,* XIV, n. 12; S. C. C. in *Novarien. Iuris administrandi Sacramenta,* 17 dec. 1691—Pallottini, s. v. *De Parocho,* XIV, n. 18.

[36] S. C. C., *Derthonen.,* 19 nov., 3 dec. 1718—*Fontes,* n. 3177; S. C. C., *Derthonen.,* 7 dec. 1720—*Fontes,* n. 3217.

[37] S. C. C., *Eugubina Iura parochialia,* 2 apr. 1729—Pallottini, s. v. *De Parocho,* XIV, n. 17.

the nearest parish priest should administer the sacraments to him. However, the pastor could choose another priest.[38]

5. To the *"beneficiati"* of a parish who had left their own parish limits. They received extreme unction and Holy Viaticum from the parish priest in whose parish limits they became ill.[39]

6. As to hospitals within parish limits and the pastor's jurisdiction over them, Drumm presented the following conclusion:

> The Council of Trent, in reforming the organization of the parishes, passed rigorous laws insisting both on the territorial and on the personal relationship of the faithful to their respective parish priests. By the common law, therefore, pastors were responsible for the care of their sick in hospitals. This strict enactment was frequently somewhat modified as regards large hospitals serving many parishes, (1) by exemption granted through particular law to hospitals of exempt religious; (2) by Papal privilege; (3) by custom. The status of chaplains in these institutions depended, consequently, on the nature of the hospital itself, its privileges, and on established customs in individual cases.[40]

Regarding the exemption of hospitals by law the following should be noted. Hospitals were always placed in the same category in law as non-exempt religious houses of men or women, colleges, orphan asylums, and similar institutions.[41]

By their very nature hospitals which were meant primarily for externs could not be included in the class of institutions exempt by law. Thus by pre-Code law a hospital for externs when operated by exempt clerics as a part of their house was not withdrawn from the jurisdiction of the local parish priest with reference to the extern patients quartered in the hospital.[42]

---

[38] *De Officio et Potestate Parochi Descriptio,* Pars II, cap. 22, n. 2.

[39] S. C. C., *Mantuana,* 16 mart. 1680—*Fontes,* n. 2854.

[40] *Hospital Chaplains,* The Catholic University of America Canon Law Studies, n. 178 (Washington, D. C.: The Catholic University of America Press, 1943), p. 29.

[41] S. C. Ep. et Reg., 3 sept. 1865—*Acta Sanctae Sedis* (41 vols., Romae, 1865-1908), III (1868), 653 (hereafter cited as *ASS*).

[42] Some orders, however, enjoyed exemption by apostolic privilege in favor of their dependents, e.g., the Barnabites. Cf. S. C. de Ep. et Reg., 21 iul. 1848—Bizzarri, p. 583.

Exempt religious who maintained their own infirmaries for solely their own members could not be said to have hospitals in the ordinary usage of the word. These infirmaries were to be classed as private sanitariums; they were hospitals in only a broad sense. In a case such as this the exemption which was enjoyed by the religious, and therefore also by the priest who was deputed to look after them, extended naturally to their infirmary. If the religious community was exempt from episcopal jurisdiction, *a fortiori* it was also exempt from parochial subjection.[43]

As the result of a litigation between the hospital of St. Euphemia in Rome and the parish of SS. Cosmas and Damian, the Sacred Congregation of Bishops and Regulars set down the following points: (1) the pastor has jurisdiction, established in law, over those who have a domicile within the limits of the parish; (2) this parochial right extends even over pious houses, and it does not cease to exist unless the institute is exempt by its very nature, by special privilege, or by centenary or immemorial custom; (3) whenever there is question of precluding the exercise of parochial rights, a strict interpretation must be adhered to, and hence those privileges which by what they grant deviate from the common law are not to be extended as applicable to corollaries flowing from them.[44]

With reference to the matter of exemption by way of papal privilege, Drumm noted that the hospitals of religious orders to which exemption from parochial care had been granted surpassed at one time all other exempt foundations. Bouix (1808-1870) claimed that formerly the majority of hospitals throughout Europe possessed this status of exemption.[45]

Drumm stated in his conclusion:

> Through custom at least the right of the local ordinary also to exempt institutional chaplains in whole or in part

---

[43] Conc. Trident., sess. XXV, *de ref.*, c. 11.

[44] S. C. de Ep. et Reg., 21 iul. 1876—*ASS*, X (1877), 405; cf. Drumm, *Hospital Chaplains*, pp. 21-22.

[45] Cf. *Hospital Chaplains*, p. 22; *Tractatus de Parocho* (3. ed., Parisiis, 1880), p. 653.

from the jurisdiction of the parish priest was confirmed by a decision of the Roman Curia.[46]

The provision was that there should be present a grave reason and that the exemption should be granted with the observing of the necessary formalities of notifying the local pastor concerned or of issuing a decree.

In the absence (1) of such a decree, (2) of exemption by law, (3) of Papal privilege, (4) of immemorial custom, the chaplains of these hospitals in the care of souls were either (1) formal vicars of the parish priest or (2) auxiliary priests deputed by the bishop to administer the sacraments through express or tacit agreement with the parish priest. Their rights and obligations were dependent on these various factors.[47]

7. As to colleges, orphan asylums, prisons, and non-exempt religious houses of men and women, the parish priest had the same jurisdiction over their inhabitants as he had over those of hospitals, since all the above mentioned institutions were placed in the same category as the hospitals. Therefore, what has already been stated about the status of hospitals applied to those institutions also. Decisions at one time favored the parochial rights of the local parish priests, and at another time the rights of the institutions' chaplains.[48]

In conclusion to the foregoing remarks on the licit ministry of the pastor it should be noted that, throughout the centuries after the Council of Trent, the Roman instructions and the encyclicals of the various Pontiffs as well as the decisions of the Roman Curia emphasized the rights of the parish priest over his subjects as

---

[46] "Per Ordinarii decretum, dummodo graves adsint rationes, etiam conservatoria a iurisdictione parochiali eximi posse."—S. C. C., 2 ian. 1873—*ASS,* VIII (1874), 546.

[47] *Hospital Chaplains,* p. 29.

[48] S. C. C., *Romana,* 27 aug. 1667—*Fontes,* n. 2802; S. C. C. in *Mediolanen. Iurium parochialium,* 28 iul. 1705—*Fontes,* n. 2996; S. C. C. in *Astens. Iurium parochialium,* 27 nov. 1717—Pallottini, s. v. *De Parocho,* XIV, n. 34; S. C. C. in *Praenestina administrationis Sacramentorum,* 22 mart. 1823—Pallottini, s. v. *De Parocho,* XIV, n. 29; S. C. Ep. et Reg., *Parmen.,* 21 iul. 1848—Bizzarri, p. 583.

to the administration of the last sacraments. They also warned the religious of the illicitness of their ministry if the latter proceeded without the pastor's permission.[49]

Barbosa pointed out that an excommunicated pastor could not distribute the Holy Eucharist in church, nor could he carry it to the sick. A pastor who acted contrary to this norm sinned gravely and incurred an irregularity. However, Barbosa added that in extreme necessity an excommunicated pastor could administer Holy Viaticum to a dying person, if no other priest was available.[50]

By reason of his office the pastor was obliged *ex iustitia* to administer the last sacraments. Therefore, any wilful neglect or inexcusable delay was considered a grave sin.[51]

If a parochial church had become incorporated with an Order either *pleno iure* or *plenissimo iure,* then the care of souls of all the faithful not exempted from parochial jurisdiction became the right of the regular parochial priest who was rightly appointed there by his religious superior. Everyone enumerated above, if he continued to be subject to parochial jurisdiction, was to receive the sacraments from his regular pastor.[52]

B. Superiors of Clerical Exempt Religious

Regulars, since they were exempt from episcopal jurisdiction, were *a fortiori* exempt from parochial jurisdiction also.[53] Consequently the superior of a clerical exempt religious house, and not the parish priest, administered the last sacraments licitly to all those who were under his jurisdiction.

[49] Benedictus XIV, ep. encycl. *Inter omnigenas,* 2 febr. 1744—*Fontes,* n. 339; Innocentius X, const. *Cum sicut,* 14 maii 1648, par. 4, sect. 1-17—*Fontes,* n. 232; Pius IX (1846-1878) declared *ipso facto* excommunicated with reservation to the Holy See those religious who presumed to minister extreme unction or Viaticum to clerics or to lay people without the pastor's permission—Const. *Apostolicae Sedis,* 12 oct. 1869, II, n. 14—*Fontes,* n. 552; S. C. de Prop. Fide, 13 iunii 1633—*Fontes,* n. 4450, S. C. C., *Ripana,* 3 febr. 1652—Pallottini, s. v. *De Parocho,* XIV, n. 33; S. C. C. in *Monopolitana Iuris sepeliendi,* 24 sept. 1670—Pallottini, s. v. *De Parocho,* XIV, n. 33.

[50] *De Officio et Potestate Parochi Descriptio,* Pars II, cap. 20, n. 5.

[51] *Ibid.,* cap. 22, n. 10.

[52] Schmalzgrueber, *Ius Ecclesiasticum Universum,* Lib. III, tit. 37, nn. 4-5.

[53] Conc. Trident. sess. XXV, *de ref.,* c. 11.

The following were under such a superior's jurisdiction:

1. The professed members of the monastery, the lay brothers, and the novices. The superior had the right of licitly administering the last sacraments to these three groups. Any other priest, whether regular or secular, needed the superior's permission before he could licitly minister to any sick member of the monastery.[54]

2. The oblates (*donati*) and those who worked and resided within the monastery. The superior could licitly administer the last sacraments to these persons, provided that the pastor himself did not vindicate the right to himself. The superior could not reject the pastor's request.[55]

3. The household servants (*familiares*) of the monastery. These could receive the last sacraments from the superior under the condition mentioned in the preceding paragraph. However, before the members of this group could at all receive the last sacraments from the superior, they had to qualify as being true household members of the monastery.

The Council of Trent and Pope Gregory XIII (1572-1585) postulated the following qualifications: 1) the *familiares* had to be in the actual service of the monastery; 2) they had to reside within the monastic premises; and 3) they had to live under obedience to the regulars, not indeed in the sense of being bound by the vow of religious obedience, but in the sense that they owed the same obedience that a child owes to its parents.[56]

That these three conditions were deemed essential is evident from later decisions of the Sacred Congregation of the Council. In 1738 an abbot of the Praemonstratensian Order was refused the right to administer the sacraments to those laypeople who worked in the monastery, but lived away from its premises. Yet, permission was granted to administer to those residing within the monastery limits.[57] And in another decision it was decreed that

---

[54] Barbosa, *De Officio et Potestate Parochi Descriptio,* Pars II, cap. 22, n. 4; Zitelli, *Apparatus Iuris Ecclesiastici,* Lib. III, art. 5, n. 374.

[55] Barbosa, *loc. cit.*

[56] Conc. Trident. sess. XXIV, *de ref.,* cap. 11; const. *Circumspecta,* 25 nov. 1580—*Bull. Rom.,* IV, 454-456.

[57] S. C. C. in *Vratislavien. Iurium parochialium,* 25 ian. 1738—*Thesaurus Resolutionum Sacrae Congregationis Concilii* (167 vols., Romae, 1718-1908), VIII, 17.

the religious could not minister to those persons who happened to be in a hospital located within the limits of the monastery, unless they were household members of the monastery. The right of administration belonged to the proper pastor.[58]

4. Nuns and the domestics who had residence in a building connected with the monastery. Before the Council of Trent as well as after the Council, nuns enjoyed the same privileges and favors as the regulars to whom they were subject. Consequently nuns were exempt from the parochial jurisdiction of the local pastor. It is not certain whether the abbot or his delegated substitute had a precedent right over the confessors in administering the sacraments. It is certain, however, that the nuns and the resident domestics were free from the jurisdiction of the local pastor.[59]

C. The Minister for the Bishop

Although the bishop resided within the limits of some parish, nevertheless the last sacraments could not be administered by the local pastor.[60]. It was the highest dignitary of the cathedral chapter who ministered the sacraments to the sick bishop.[61]

Section 3. The Rite in Which the Sacraments Were Administered

Concerning the rite in which the last sacraments had to be administered, Pius X (1903-1914) declared that Holy Viaticum had to be given to the dying person according to his proper rite, and by his proper pastor. However, in urgent necessity any priest could administer the sacrament, but in the priest's own rite.[62]

---

[58] S. C. C. in *Asten.*, 27 nov. 1717—Pallottini, s. v. *De Parocho*, XIV, n. 34.

[59] Cf. S. C. C. in *Occident.*, 22 nov. 1721—*Fontes*, n. 3234; S. C. C. in *Ulyxbonen. Occidentalis*, 17 sept. 1722—*Fontes*, n. 3247; S. C. Ep. et Reg., *Caesenaten.*, mense maio 1788—*Fontes*, n. 1881; S. C. C. in *Dubium administrationis Sacramentorum*, 7 et 28 aug. 1683—*Fontes*, n. 2872.

[60] S. C. C. in *Firmana Iurium parochialium*, 4 aug. 1685—Pallottini, s. v. *De Parocho*, XIV, n. 21.

[61] S. C. C. in *Faventina Praeeminentiarum et Funerum*, 7 iun. 1760, Pallottini, s. v. *De Parocho*, XIV, n. 22.

[62] Const. *Tradita ab antiquis*, 14 sept. 1912, n. 5—*Fontes*, n. 698.

The Sacred Congregation for the Propagation of the Faith decreed that Latin missionaries could not administer the sacraments to Catholics of the Oriental rite, except in the absence of the proper pastor, or when, notwithstanding the presence of the pastor, the Oriental Catholic would find difficulty in receiving the sacraments from his own pastor. In the case of urgent necessity the Latin missionaries were obliged to administer Holy Viaticum and extreme unction in their own rite.[63]

---

[63] S. C. de Prop. Fide, 11 oct. 1780—*Fontes,* n. 4584.

CHAPTER III

The Minister of Last Confession

Can. 882—In periculo mortis omnes sacerdotes, licet ad confessiones non approbati, valide et licite absolvunt quoslibet poenitentes a quibusvis peccatis aut censuris, quantumvis reservatis et notoriis, etiamsi praesens sit sacerdos approbatus, salvo praescripto can. 884, 2252.

Article 1. The Danger of Death

The Council of Trent had legislated that any person who was in immediate danger of death could be absolved both validly and licitly from any sin or censure by any validly ordained priest.[1] The present canon merely requires the presence of the danger of death. For the use of the canon the danger need not be immediate, which condition of immediacy was required by the Council of Trent.

Properly considered the phrase *in periculo mortis* differs in meaning from the expression *in articulo mortis.* A prudent fear that death will soon occur is connoted by the expression *in periculo mortis,* whereas the latter phrase signifies that an imminent and inevitable danger of death is with moral certainty known to be present. Canonists and theologians, however, have come to regard the two phrases as synonymous.[2] The Holy See has repeatedly

[1] Sess. XIV, *de sanctissimo poenitentiae sacramento,* can. 6-7.

[2] Cf. St. Alphonsus, *Theologia Moralis* (3 vols., Augustae Taurinorum, 1891), Lib. VI, nn. 560-561—Vol. II, 442; De Lugo, *Disputationes Scholasticae et Morales* (editio nova, 8 vols., Parisiis: apud Ludovicum Vivés, 1868-1869), *De Sacramento Poenitentiae,* Disp. XVIII, sect. 21—Vol. V, 171; Cappello, *Summa Iuris Canonici* (3 vols., Vol. II, 4. ed., Romae: Apud Aedes Universitatis Gregorianae, 1945), II, 204; *Tractatus Canonico-Moralis de Sacramentis* (3 vols. in 6, Romae: Domus Editorialis Marietti, 1935-1945; Vol. I, 4. ed., 1945; Vol. II, pars I, 4. ed., 1944; Vol. II, pars II, 2. ed., 1942; Vol. II, pars III, 1935; Vol. III, partes I et II, 4. ed., 1939), II pars I, 266; Coronata, *Institutiones Iuris Canonici ad usum utriusque cleri et scholarum de Sacramentis* (3 vols., Romae: Domus Editorialis Marietti, 1943-1946), I, 357-358 (hereafter cited as *De Sacramentis*).

used the two phrases promiscuously, so that in most instances they have the same force.[3]

To use the faculty granted by canon 882, therefore, it is not necessary that the penitent be on the very brink of the grave. It suffices that the priest have a prudent fear that the penitent may die within a short time. If persons could avail themselves of this canon only at the moment of death, then it could be said that the Church placed a rather rigorous condition for the use of it. Many persons being so close to death would be unable to make a confession. The privilege in many instances would be useless. The Church, therefore, solicitous for the spiritual welfare of its faithful, particularly at the end of life, postulates simply that there be a danger of death.

Canon 209 supplies jurisdiction to a priest who doubts whether or not the danger of death is present. Under such circumstances he may validly and licitly absolve from any sin or censure, as long as he can judge that the danger of death (not necessarily death itself) is at least probable. Likewise, if the confessor falsely judges that the danger of death is present, when it really is not, the absolution is still certainly valid, and if administered in good faith also licit, in virtue of the same canon 209.[4]

This danger of death may arise from an intrinsic cause such as a sickness, an inflicted wound, a difficult birth, extreme old age, etc. An extrinsic cause, such as the waging of war, a dangerous sea trip, a surgical operation, a severe pain, etc., may likewise constitute a danger of death. Since this danger of death need be merely probable, many groups of the faithful may avail themselves of confessing to any confessor. For example, the Sacred Penitentiary decreed in 1915 that mobilized soldiers are to be considered as being in danger of death.[5]

In regard to the dangers of war Pope Pius XII through the

---

[3] S.C.S. Off. (Kentucky), 10 maii 1821—*Fontes,* n. 860; S.C.S. Off. (Cincinnat.), 13 sept. 1859—*Fontes,* n. 955; Pius IX, const. *Apostolicae Sedis,* 12 oct, 1869, I, n. 12—*Fontes,* n. 552.

[4] Cf. James Kelly, *The Jurisdiction of the Simple Confessor,* The Catholic University of America Canon Law Studies, n. 43 (Washington, D. C.: The Catholic University of America, 1927), pp. 77-78.

[5] 29 maii—*AAS,* VII (1915), 282.

Sacred Consistory decreed that before an imminent battle, or if a battle has already begun, the priest may licitly absolve every soldier from all sins and censures, although reserved and notorious, with the general formula or the common absolution, apart from a previous oral confession. Under these same circumstances Holy Viaticum can be administered too. Pope Pius XII granted to the priests permission also to absolve licitly by means of a general absolution and to grant the Apostolic Blessing to all the faithful who during a war happened to dwell in the so-called open or free cities and at the moment were actually exposed to air bombings.[6] Of course the proper dispositions, namely, the intention of making an integral confession at the earliest possible time, and the eliciting of an act of contrition were necessary requisites on the part of the penitent before he could avail himself of the above mentioned privilege. Before the priest could use the privilege he had to be confronted by a large number of soldiers or residents of these open cities, and time had to be wanting for the hearing of the confessions of all of them individually.

Since great progress has been made in the means of travel, it can be said safely that an airplane trip in itself without any accompanying aggravating circumstances as well as a boat trip are not perilous. A submarine trip may perhaps constitute a danger to life, but in view of the recent modern progress which has been made on this craft it cannot be stated absolutely as being perilous. All these causes are viewed under peaceful conditions. In the midst of an attack all would be perilous.[7]

ARTICLE 2. THE CONFESSOR

For the granting of a valid absolution two factors are postulated, namely, the possession of the power of orders, and the holding of either an ordinary or a delegated jurisdiction over the penitent.[8] In danger of death all priests, though not approved for the hearing of confessions, can validly and licitly absolve any penitent from any sins or censures, even if an approved priest is present. Here the

[6] 8 dec. 1939—*AAS,* XXXI (1939), 711-712.

[7] Cf. Cappello, *Summa Iuris Canonici,* II, 204.

[8] Canons 871; 872.

jurisdiction over the dying penitent is delegated to the confessor by the law itself. Hence, although a priest may lack jurisdiction for the hearing of confessions under ordinary circumstances, nevertheless that same impeded priest receives the necessary jurisdiction from the law itself to hear anyone's confession when the latter is in danger of death. Whether the priest be under the penalty of an excommunication, a suspension or an interdict; whether he be irregular or for other reasons be not approved for the hearing of confessions; whether he be a heretic, a schismatic, reduced to the lay state or degraded, still by virtue of canon 882 such a priest has the faculty to hear the confession of anyone dangerously close to death. In order that a penitent may receive every possible opportunity to have his sins and censures absolved before death, the Church removes every restriction on the minister.

De Lugo (1583-1660) and Ballerini (1805-1881) set up an order in which the confessors should be called to the penitent. According to their order an approved confessor of the proper diocese should approach the penitent before any other confessor. If he is not available, then an approved confessor of another diocese should be called. In his absence a priest without any jurisdiction, a *sacerdos simplex,* should be preferred to a suspended or an interdicted priest. An irregular should be preferred to an excommunicate, an excommunicate to a *vitandus,* a *vitandus* should be preferred to a degraded priest, and a degraded priest to a heretic. Only as a last resort could a schismatic be summoned. However, the observance of this order of confessors is not of precept. The Code does not set up any particular order which anyone must follow in summoning a confessor for an urgent case.[9]

The following statements form the common teaching of canonists and theologians on the minister of confession in cases of danger of death.[10]

---

[9] De Lugo, *Disputationes Scholasticae et Morales, De Sacramento Poenitentiae,* Disp. XVIII, sect. 35—Vol. V, 173-174. Ballerini, *Opus Theologicum Morale* (Absolvit et edidit Dominicus Palmieri, 7 vols., Prati, 1889-1893), *De Sacramento Poenitentiae,* Sect. V, cap. 2, n. 592—Vol. V, 295-296.

[10] Cf. De Lugo, *Disputationes Scholasticae et Morales, De Sacramento Poenitentiae,* Disp. XVIII, sect. 18 sq.—Vol. V, 169 sq.; A. Lehmkuhl, *Theologia Moralis* (14. ed., 2 vols., Friburgi Brisgoviae, 1914), II, n. 72,

1. An excommunicated confessor, although a *vitandus,* or a suspended, or a personally interdicted confessor, can validly and licitly absolve a penitent in danger of death, even if another priest is present.[11]

2. A non-approved confessor can validly and licitly absolve a penitent although an approved confessor is present. Kelly has stated that if a priest without faculties to hear confessions would grant absolution in danger of death when an approved priest is present, "he would seem to commit a light sin, at any rate, by violating the order of preference demanded by natural equity."[12]

Moriarty refuted this statement by saying:

> This is not at all present. It attaches a note of inherent illicitness to any use of canon 882 by a priest without faculties in the presence of an approved priest. But the canon simply states that the absolution in such a case is both valid and licit. Whatever may have been the purpose of the legislator in formulating this canon, whether it was to provide most carefully for the salvation of souls by precluding any hesitation or doubt of action on the part of the minister because of a question of illicit-

p. 42; Marc et Gestermann, *Institutiones Morales Alphonsianae* (18. ed., 2 vols., Lugduni et Lutetiae Parisiorum, 1927), II, n. 1760, 2, p. 294; Piscetta-Gennaro, *Elementa Theologiae Moralis* (7 vols., Vol. V, 6. ed., Torino: Società Editrice Internazionale, 1946), V, n. 652, pp. 516-517; Cappello, *De Sacramentis,* II, pars I, 266; Coronata, *De Sacramentis,* I, 359.

[11] Cf. canon 2261, §§ 1, 3: Prohibetur excommunicatus licite Sacramenta et Sacramentalia conficere et ministrare, salvis exceptionibus quae sequuntur. Sed ab excommunicatis vitandis necnon ab aliis excommunicatis, postquam intercesserit sententia condemnatoria aut declaratoria, fideles in solo mortis periculo possunt petere tum absolutionem sacramentalem ad normam can. 882, 2252, tum etiam, si alii desint ministri, cetera Sacramenta et Sacramentalia. Canon 2284: Si incursa fuerit censura suspensionis quae vetat administrationem Sacramentorum et Sacramentalium, servetur praescriptum can. 2261; si censura suspensionis quae prohibet actum iurisdictionis in foro seu interno seu externo, actus est invalidus, ex. gr., absolutio sacramentalis, si lata sit sententia condemnatoria vel declaratoria, aut Superior expresse declaret se ipsam iurisdictionis potestatem revocare; secus est illicitus tantum, nisi a fidelibus petitus fuerit ad normam mem. can. 2261, § 2. Canon 2275, 2°: Personaliter interdicti prohibentur Sacramenta et Sacramentalia ministrare, conficere et recipere, ad normam can. 2260, § 1; 2261.

[12] *The Jurisdiction of the Simple Confessor,* p. 93.

> ness, or whether there was any other reason that prompted the concession, the canon as it stands clearly indicates that the absolution is not only valid but also licit. Consequently, any illicitness in the use of the faculties of canon 882 will not arise *per se,* from the nature of the case, but rather *per accidens;* for example, if absolution were given in a noticeable manner before bystanders by a priest who is a public apostate, or by one dressed as a layman, when the absolution could be given by another priest without such danger.[13]

In the writer's opinion, Moriarty's view is the more convincing one.

3. If a penitent close to death cannot confess without great difficulty or repugnance to another confessor who may be present, he can licitly confess to an apostate, schismatic or heretic priest. And the same priest can validly and licitly absolve such a penitent. It must be remembered, however, that beyond the cases of necessity a communication *in divinis* with an apostate, a heretic, or a schismatic is illicit. Before summoning these priests to a dying penitent the possibility of scandal and perversion must be seriously considered. The communication *in divinis* with such confessors may even in circumstances of urgent necessity appear to some of the faithful as a profession of a false sect. The approach of such a priest may also cause the penitent to lose his own faith through the efforts of an erring priest. Absolution by an apostate, schismatic, or heretic is always valid and *per se* also licit. *Per accidens* it can be illicit in consequence of the probable presence of scandal or of the fear of perversion.

Some authors advise that in practice a penitent would do better to elicit an act of contrition and trust in God's infinite mercy,

---

[13] *The Extraordinary Absolution from Censures,* The Catholic University of America Canon Law Studies, n. 113 (Washington, D. C.: The Catholic University of America Press, 1938), p. 76; Kelly later, in "Faculties of Absolving and Dispensing in Danger of Death," *The Ecclesiastical Review* (*The American Ecclesiastical Review,* Vols. I-XXXII, Philadelphia, 1889-1905; from 1905: *The Ecclesiastical Review,* Vols. XXXIII-CIX, Philadelphia, 1905-1943); from 1944: *The American Ecclesiastical Review,* Vol. CX, 1944, Washington, D. C., LXXXV (1931), 257, revised his wording to read: ". . . he would seem to commit at most a light sin. . . ."

rather than to expose himself to the danger of losing his faith by calling a fallen-away priest.[14]

A priest without faculties could avail himself of the prerogative granted in canon 882, even if he could easily receive from a competent superior the faculty for absolving.[15] In danger of death all reservation ceases, and the Church grants jurisdiction to every priest who does not already have jurisdiction.[16] In cases, however, in which the penitent is obliged to have recourse after recovery, De Meester advised that a priest who already possesses the postulated faculties in a particular case should absolve rather than a priest who obtains the needed faculties only in consequence of the existing emergency.[17] But the supposition of the presence of such a favored priest is hardly practical, for it will be extremely rare that a priest will have the faculties to absolve from *ab homine* incurred censures, from censures reserved *specialissimo modo*, or from the specific case listed in canon 2388, § 1, which has become reserved exclusively to the Sacred Penitentiary. These are the only cases in which recourse is prescribed after recovery from the danger of death.

In absolving from the sins and censures the priest should absolve a penitent first from the excommunication or personal interdict, since the presence of either of these two censures prevents the licit reception of the sacraments. Authors point out that, though the confessor's antecedent absolution of the sins would be valid, nevertheless, his willful inversion of the order in absolving would be gravely illicit.[18] However, if a person is suspended, the

---

[14] Cf. Ferreres, *Compendium Theologiae Moralis* (14. ed., 2 vols., Barcinone, 1928), II, nn. 648, 651, pp. 352, 356; Noldin-Schmitt, *Summa Theologiae Moralis iuxta Codicem Iuris Canonici* (26. ed., 3 vols., Oeniponte/Lipsiae: Felician Rauch, 1940), III, par. 43, sect. 3, b, p. 42.

[15] Cappello, *De Censuris iuxta Codicem Iuris Canonici* (Augustae Taurinorum: Marietti, 1919), n. 114, 2; Cerato, *Censurae Vigentes Ipso Facto a Codice Iuris Canonici Excerptae* (2. ed., Patavii, 1921), p. 40.

[16] Cf. Cerato, *Censurae Vigentes Ipso Facto a Codice Iuris Canonici Excerptae*, p. 40.

[17] *Juris Canonici et Juris Canonico-Civilis Compendium* (nova ed., 3 vols. in 4, Brugis: Desclée De Brouwer et Sii, 1921-1928), III, pars I, 180.

[18] Cf. canons 2246, § 3; 2250, § 1; 2275, 2°; 2260, § 1; Cappello, *De Censuris iuxta Codicem Iuris Canonici*, nn. 106, 107, 147, 465; Cerato, *Censurae Vigentes Ipso Facto a Codice Iuris Canonici Excerptae*, p. 33; Moriarty, *The Extraordinary Absolution from Censures*, p. 78.

confessor may grant absolution for the suspension either before or after he grants absolution from the sins, for a suspension does not impede the licit reception of the sacraments.[19]

Oriental priests may avail themselves of the prerogative granted in canon 882, since this canon certainly concerns the good of souls, and according to the principles of Canon Law and Theology no distinction is to be made between Catholics of the Latin and Oriental rites in this respect.

ARTICLE 3. THE CONFESSOR'S POWER

Canon 882 grants the confessor the power to absolve from any sin or censure. If the person in danger of death is baptized and has the proper dispositions, he can be absolved from any censure whether it be single or multiple, occult, public, or notorious. Whether the censure be an excommunication, a suspension, or an interdict, whether *latae* or *ferendae sententiae, ab homine* or *a iure,* sustained before a declaratory sentence has been passed or inflicted only upon a previous condemnatory sentence, it can, by virtue of canon 882, be absolved in cases where danger of death is present. In addition, censures reserved either to the ordinary, to the Holy See, even *specialissimo modo,* or personally to the Pope, can be remitted.

Genicot (1856-1900)-Salsmans (1873-1944) and Jone expressed the opinion that a suspension, since it actually does not impede the licit reception of the sacraments, cannot be absolved through the use of this canon.[20] The canon, however, makes no exception with reference to suspension; it makes no restriction whatsoever either on the sins which can be absolved or on the censures. The absolution of every kind of a censure seems certainly to be authorized by the ruling of this canon. Nearly all the recent authors are of this opinion.[21]

---

[19] Cf. canons 2250, § 1; 2278, § 1; Cerato, *op. cit.,* p. 33.

[20] *Institutiones Theologiae Moralis* (11. ed., 2 vols., Bruxellis: Dewit, 1927), II, n. 332; "Die Absolutionsvollmachten in Todesgefahr," *Theologische-praktische Quartalschift* LXXIX (1926), 16.

[21] Cf. Cappello, *De Sacramentis,* II, pars I, 266; De Meester, *Juris Canonici et Juris Canonico-Civilis Compendium,* III, pars II, 180-181; Kelly, *The Jurisdiction of the Simple Confessor,* pp. 94-95; Moriarty, *The Extraordinary Absolution from Censures,* pp. 84-85.

Notice should be taken of the fact that the Code makes no provision for the dispensation of vindictive penalties or irregularities. No provision is made whereby the confessor may lift these by means of a dispensation that may be granted in danger of death. Only those norms which regulate the possible remission of vindictive penalties and irregularities in urgent cases when the danger of scandal or infamy is present may be applied in the danger of death in so far as the postulated conditions exist. Since only the reception and the exercise of ecclesiastical orders are prevented by irregularities, the case in which a dispensation in danger of death will be of any use is extremely rare.[22]

Moriarty offers an example of the need of dispensing from an irregularity when the danger of death has arisen from an extrinsic cause. A military chaplain, about to set out for war, is affected with an occult irregularity which prevents him from saying Mass. In such a case, if the ordinary cannot be reached, and if there is a probability that the chaplain's reputation will suffer as a consequence of his not saying Mass, any confessor can dispense from that irregularity, and the priest may then exercise his orders. In this particular case, however, it should be remembered that the dispensation could not be granted if notice of the irregularity had been brought to the judicial forum, or if the priest had contracted the irregularity because of voluntary homicide, or effective abortion, or of cooperation in either of these two crimes.[23]

In like manner, if the chaplain incurred a vindictive *latae sententiae* penalty and no declaratory sentence has been pronounced, he is excused from observing the penalty if in doing so he would sacrifice his good repute, and in the external forum no one can exact from him the observance of this penalty as long as it is not notorious.[24] In the same case, likewise, if the *latae sententiae* vindictive penalty is occult and there is danger of scandal or infamy from the observance of it, e.g., in a vindictive suspension, then the confessor can suspend the obligation of observing the penalty or can dispense from it according to the norms of canon 2290.

[22] Cf. canons 2290; 990; Kelly, *The Jurisdiction of the Simple Confessor*, p. 80; Moriarty, *The Extraordinary Absolution from Censures*, p. 85.

[23] Cf. canons 990, §§ 1 & 2; 985, 4°.

[24] Cf. canon 2232, § 1.

Moriarty states that if the conditions concerning the remission of vindictive penalties and irregularities in urgent cases are verified in a case of danger of death, there is no reason why the norms should not be applied in danger of death.[25]

Finally, if for having attempted marriage a priest has in consequence of the ruling in canon 2388, § 1, become excommunicated, but thereon is prevented for very serious reasons from leaving the woman in the event of his recovery, so that he must continue to live with her, he can be given absolution on condition that his continued life with the woman has been determined by him to follow the pattern of a brother and sister relationship, but there rests on him the obligation of making recourse to the Sacred Penitentiary after his recovery from the danger of death.[26]

ARTICLE 4. THE CONDITIONS

Canon 884 states that a priest's absolution of his accomplice *in peccato turpi* is invalid except in danger of death, and that even in danger of death such an absolution is illicit outside the case of necessity. If any priest other than the priest-accomplice can hear the confession of the dying person without danger of grave infamy to the two accomplices or of scandal to others, and the penitent does not refuse to confess to this other priest, then the case of necessity is not considered to be present. A priest who would absolve his accomplice *in peccato turpi* from the sin of complicity in such circumstances would indeed grant absolution validly, but his action would be gravely illicit. Through his commission of such a sin he would incur the *latae sententiae specialissimo modo* reserved excommunication which the law has enacted as a penalty for the *absolutio complicis*.[27]

---

[25] *The Extraordinary Absolution from Censures*, p. 86.

[26] Cf. Moriarty, *op. cit.*, p. 86; S. Poenit., decr. 18 apr. 1936—*AAS*, XXVIII (1936), 242, 243; declar. 4 maii 1937—*AAS*, XXIX (1937), 283, 284.

[27] Canon 2367, § 1: Absolvens vel fingens absolvere complicem in peccato turpi incurrit ipso facto in excommunicationem specialissimo modo Sedi Apostolicae reservatam; idque etiam in mortis articulo, si alius sacerdos, licet non approbatus ad confessiones, sine gravi aliqua exoritura infamia et scandalo, possit excipere morientis confessionem, excepto casu quo moribundus recuset alii confiteri.

The case here presented constitutes the single exception in which the possibility of a licit absolution has been excluded by the legislator, and it receives express mention in canon 882 in the phrase "*salvo praescripto can. 884*."[28]

Appended to canon 882 is the phrase "*salvo praescripto can. 2252*." Canon 2252 prescribes that, when anyone in danger of death has been absolved from an *ab homine* inflicted censure, or from a censure reserved *specialissimo modo* to the Holy See, by a confessor who lacks special faculties for such cases, he is obliged to make recourse within one month after he has convalesced, and indeed under pain of reincurring the censure, to the one who inflicted the censure if it was incurred *ab homine,* or to the Sacred Penitentiary, or to someone who has the needed faculties in the case wherein the censure was incurred *a iure;* he is furthermore obliged to obey the issued mandates. But the obligation to make recourse is in no way set as an essential condition for the absolution.

Concerning this canon only two points will be stressed. First, the canon does not explicitly demand that the confessor impose this obligation upon the penitent or inform him of it. It is generally agreed that the confessor in consequence of any inherent duty of office is not bound to impose this obligation on the penitent in danger of death, but that it is left to his prudence either to inform the penitent or to remain silent about the obligation.[29]

Although strictly the confessor is not bound to demand the instituting of a recourse, at times he can and should impose the obligation of making recourse. If, however, the penitent is actually dying, the confessor should not inform him of the obligation to make recourse. Again, if the confessor prudently fears that the information will disturb the penitent, or if he at least doubts whether

[28] Cf. Kelly, *The Jurisdiction of the Simple Confessor*, pp. 80-81; Moriarty, *The Extraordinary Absolution from Censures,* p. 74.

[29] Cf. Cerato, *Censurae Vigentes Ipso Facto a Codice Iuris Canonici Excerptae*, p. 42; Cappello, *De Censuris iuxta Codicem Iuris Canonici*, n. 116; Coronata, *Institutiones Iuris Canonici ad usum utriusque Cleri et Scholarum* (2. ed., 5 vols., Taurini; Marietti, 1939-1947), IV, n. 1760, pp. 183-184; Kelly, *The Jurisdiction of the Simple Confessor,* p. 81; Moriarty, *The Extraordinary Absolution from Censures,* pp. 90-91.

it will be of benefit to the penitent, he may omit all mention about the making of the recourse; if he foresees that the penitent's ratification of the obligation to make recourse will be to the advantage of the penitent, he should inform the penitent of his obligation to make recourse.

Moriarty is of the opinion that it does not appear to be correct to say that for circumstantial reasons the confessor may be bound in most cases to impose the obligation of recourse, inasmuch as otherwise the penitent, at least if he is a layman, would never know of the obligation. It may be presumed that if the penitent is a priest he will know of the obligation of recourse without being informed. But whether he be a priest or a layman, it seems that the confessor should follow the norms stated above.[30]

Secondly, all authors admit that a confessor, if he foresees that the making of recourse after the recovery from the danger of death will be morally impossible for the penitent, can absolve the penitent without declaring the obligation of recourse, even in the case of an *ab homine* inflicted censure, or of an incurred censure which is reserved *specialissimo modo* to the Holy See. Instead the confessor himself can then impose the penance and demand the satisfaction which the penitent must within the specified time perform under pain of reincurring the same kind of censure. This is made possible by the application of the norm of canon 2254, § 3, to canon 2252.[31]

The more common opinion states that the confessor can absolve a penitent without declaring to him the obligation of recourse whenever it is seen that the making of recourse will be morally impossible within a month after the recovery from the danger of death, rather than within a month after the absolution.[32]

---

[30] Cf. *The Extraordinary Absolution from Censures*, p. 91.

[31] Cf. Cappello, *De Censuris iuxta Codicem Iuris Canonici*, n. 117; Coronata, *Institutiones Iuris Canonici ad usum utriusque Cleri et Scholarum*, IV, n. 1760, p. 184; De Meester, *Juris Canonici et Juris Canonico-Civilis Compendium*, III, pars II, 181; Kelly, *The Jurisdiction of the Simple Confessor*, p. 82; Moriarty, *The Extraordinary Absolution from Censures*, p. 120.

[32] Kelly, *The Jurisdiction of the Simple Confessor*, p. 82; Rainer, *Suspension of Clerics*, The Catholic University of America Canon Law Studies, n. 111 (Washington, D. C.: The Catholic University of America, 1937), pp. 212, 213; Moriarty, *The Extraordinary Absolution from Censures*, p. 121.

There is one exception to this procedure: The censure contracted through the *absolutio complicis in peccato turpi* can indeed be absolved in favor of the penitent who is in danger of death, but there remains for the penitent the obligation of instituting a recourse upon his recovery. The confessor can proceed in only one fashion. In granting absolution he must remind the penitent of the strict obligation of the later recourse.[33]

The absolution from sins or censures as given in the penitent's danger of death is in its effect limited to the internal forum. Therefore the absolution of a censure when given in virtue of the rulings of canon 822 and 2254, § 3, does not remove the canonical effect of the censure in the external forum. Consequently the principles which are enacted in canon 2251 are fully applicable also when absolution from a censure has been granted to a penitent when he was in the danger of death.[34]

---

[33] Cf. canon 2254, § 3.

[34] Canon 2251: Si absolutio censurae detur in foro externo, utrumque forum afficit; si in interno, absolutus, remoto scandalo, potest uti talem se habere etiam in actibus fori externi; sed nisi concessio absolutionis probetur aut saltem legitime praesumatur in foro externo, censura potest a Superioribus fori externi, quibus reus pareredebet, urgeri, donec absolutio in eodem foro habita fuerit. Cf. Coronata, *Institutiones Iuris Canonici ad usum utriusque Cleri et Scholarum,* IV, n. 1760, p. 185; Moriarty, *The Extraordinary Absolution from Censures,* pp. 87-88.

PART TWO

Canonical Commentary

CHAPTER IV

The Minister of Holy Viaticum

ARTICLE 1. INTRODUCTORY REMARKS

In an introductory manner mention is made that the Code makes a threefold distinction regarding the distribution of Holy Communion to the sick. Holy Communion administered to a person in danger of death is called Holy Viaticum. The reception of Holy Viaticum is of divine as well as of ecclesiastical precept.[1] The second distinction is the public administration of Holy Communion to the sick who are not in danger of death, but who receive the Eucharist for devotion's sake.[2] And, finally, there is the private administration of the Holy Eucharist to those who are not in danger of death.[3]

Administration of Holy Communion to the sick is public when the rites and ceremonies as prescribed in the Roman Ritual for a public administration are observed; if, however, the rites and ceremonies as prescribed in the Roman Ritual for a private administration are observed, then such an administration is private. Both the private and the public administration of Holy Viaticum are determined by the same norm. The present treatise is concerned solely with the private and public administration of Holy Viaticum.

At the outset it should be noted that, although the person who is in danger of death can receive Holy Viaticum repeatedly while the danger continues, nevertheless the pastoral character of the serious obligation of administering Holy Viaticum is restricted

---

[1] St. John, VI: 54; canon 864, § 1: In periculo mortis, quavis ex causa procedat, fideles sacrae communionis recipiendae precepto tenentur.

[2] Cf. canon 847: Ad infirmos publice sacra communio deferatur, nisi iusta et rationabilis causa aliud suadeat.

[3] Cf. canon 849, § 1: Communionem privatim ad infirmos quilibet sacerdos deferre potest, de venia saltem praesumpta sacerdotis, cui custodia sanctissimi Sacramenti commissa est.

to the first administration, for it is but the first reception and administration that is strictly of precept.[4] Beste, however, maintains that the pastoral character of the obligation extends to all the ministrations of Holy Viaticum while the danger of death continues.[5]

It should also be noted that, although a priest alone is the ordinary minister of the distribution of Holy Communion, and a deacon the extraordinary minister,[6] nevertheless, once the hosts are validly consecrated, there is no longer any question of validity relative to their distribution by any person. Regardless of the character of his faith and dispositions, any person can effectively serve in the instrumental capacity of distributing validly consecrated hosts.[7] The present analysis will accordingly treat of the persons who in virtue of their very office are constituted as the licit ministers of Holy Viaticum, and of the circumstances which warrant the constituted minister's licit administration of Holy Viaticum.

ARTICLE 2. THE LOCAL PASTOR

The local pastor has the duty of administering Viaticum to the persons who are in danger of death. This obligation includes both the public and the private administration of the sacrament.[8] By

[4] Cf. canon 864, §§ 1-3; Coronata, *De Sacramentis,* I, 276; Cappello, *Summa Iuris Canonici,* II, 189; Vermeersch, *Theologia Moralis* (3. ed., 4 vols., Romae: Universita Gregoriana, 1933-1937), III, 387; Davis, *Moral and Pastoral Theology* (4. ed., 4 vols., London: Sheed and Ward, 1943), III, 198-199.

[5] *Introductio in Codicem* (3. ed., Collegeville: St. John's Abbey Press, 1946), p. 230.

[6] Canon 845, § 1: Minister ordinarius sacrae communionis est solus sacerdos. § 2: Extraordinarius est diaconus, de Ordinarii loci vel parochi licentia, gravi de causa concedenda, quae in casu necessitatis legitime praesumitur.

[7] Cf. Coronata, *De Sacramentis,* I, 269; Piscetta-Gennaro, *Elementa Theologiae Moralis,* V, ante n. 516.

[8] Cf. canon 462, 3°: Functiones parocho reservatae sunt, nisi aliud iure caveatur: Sanctissimam Eucharistiam publice aut privatim tamquam Viaticum ad infirmos deferre atque in periculo mortis constitutos extrema unctione roborare. . . .

Canon 850: Sacram communionem per modum Viatici sive publice sive privatim ad infirmos deferre, pertinet ad parochum ad normam can. 848.

the term "pastor" is understood a priest or a moral person to whom has been conferred in title a parish with the care of souls to be exercised under the authority of the local ordinary.[9] In those cases, however, wherein the title of a parish is vested in a moral person, for instance, in a religious community, the moral person can at most be the parish priest in title. In such instances the moral person must provide a vicar into whose hands the actual care of souls is placed.[10]

In virtue of the ruling which is incorporated in canon 451, § 2, and as long as no more specific law has made a different provision, the following may be classified under the name of "pastor," enjoying in consequence all the rights, and subject also to all the obligations, which such a title connotes:

a) The actual vicar of a parish held in title by a moral person;[11] b) the priest who is in charge of a quasi-parish;[12] c) the substitute vicar;[13] d) the parish administrator;[14] e) the curate lawfully constituted to act as pastor when the parochial office falls vacant;[15] f) the adjutant vicar when deputed with full powers;[16] g) the assistant vicar when appointed to a parochial vicarage, if in its administration he is given full pastoral powers.[17]

The licit administration of Viaticum is reserved not merely to any pastor as such, but rather to the local pastor.[18] The pastor of the parish within the limits of which the dangerously sick person is actually present has the obligation of administering this last sacrament. Neither the domicile nor the quasi-domicile of the dying person determines the licit minister, but the place where the stricken person is actually present. If, for example, a person

---

[9] Cf. canon 451, § 1.

[10] Cf. canons 452; 471, § 4.

[11] Canon 471.

[12] Canon 216, § 3.

[13] Canons 465, § 4 and § 5; 474; 1932, § 2.

[14] Canons 472, 1°; 473.

[15] Canon 472, 2°.

[16] Canon 475.

[17] Canons 477, § 2; 1412, 1°.

[18] Canon 848, § 1: Ius et officium sacram communionem ad infirmos etiam non paroecianos extra ecclesiam deferendi pertinet ad parochum intra suum territorium.

who has a domicile in parish A, and a quasi-domicile in parish B, becomes seriously ill in parish C, the local pastor of parish C has the obligation of ministering Holy Viaticum to him. If, however, a person is stricken in his own domicile or quasi-domicile, then his proper pastor is the licit minister.[19]

Coronata states that a proper pastor could not minister Holy Viaticum to his parishioners without the proper permission of the local pastor, even if his stricken parishioners happened to be nearby in the neighboring parish. He mentions the fact that this set of circumstances frequently occurs in large cities where many neighboring parishes are established in a relatively small vicinity.[20]

At first sight there may appear to be a clash of pastors' rights and obligations regarding the administration of Holy Viaticum in those territories where two or more parishes exist, e.g., where national parishes are erected within the boundaries of the English-speaking parish. To gain a more adequate solution for this case, the essential difference between a territorial and a non-territorial parish must be noted.

A territorial parish may be defined as a sectional division which as a part of a diocese has prescribed limits within which all who have a domicile or a quasi-domicile are subject to the jurisdiction of a definitely assigned pastor, unless they happen to be exempt.[21] Affiliation with a territorial parish and the consequent jurisdictional subjection to its particular pastor depend upon the place of residence of the parishioners.[22] The pastor of a territorial parish exercises his jurisdiction over all the faithful who have a domicile

---

[19] Cf. Coronata, *De Sacramentis,* I, 275; Cappello, *De Sacramentis,* II, pars I, 265; Noldin-Schmitt, *Summa Theologiae Moralis,* III, 128; Davis, *Moral and Pastoral Theology,* III, 198.

[20] *De Sacramentis,* I, 275.

[21] Cf. Ferreres, *Institutiones Canonicae* (2. ed., 2 vols., Barcinone, 1920), I, n. 731, b; Fanfani, *De Iure Parochorum ad Normam Codicis Iuris Canonici* (Romae: Marietti, 1924), n. 3 (hereafter cited as *De Iure Parochorum*); Vermeersch-Creusen, *Epitome Iuris Canonici* (3 vols., Vol. I, 6. ed., Mechliniae: Dessain, 1937), I, n. 330; Ciesluk, *National Parishes in the United States,* The Catholic University of America Canon Law Studies, n. 190 (Washington, D. C.: The Catholic University of America Press, 1944), p. 10.

[22] Cf. canon 216, § 1.

or a quasi-domicile within the territorial limits of the parish, unless some of the faithful happen to be exempt.

A non-territorial parish receives its proper designation from the fact that the element of territory is not the primary factor in determining its existence. In the case of a non-territorial parish the factor which determines a person's affiliation with that parish is based on a personal title, and not on the objective element of domicile or of quasi-domicile. This personal title by means of which one of the faithful becomes affiliated with a non-territorial parish is the distinctive element which precludes his affiliation with the territorial parish wherein his domicile or quasi-domicile actually lies. Because of this distinctive element of a personal title non-territorial parishes are called personal parishes. The personal title may be the rite to which the person belongs (Greek, Mozarabic), and then the parish is called a parish of rite, or it may be merely the language or nationality of the person (German, Italian), and then the parish is called a national parish.

Although fundamentally a personal parish is considered without respect to territory, it can also sometimes be understood in a broader sense as a mixed personal and territorial parish. Such is the case when a personal parish extends over one or more territorial parishes, but the jurisdiction of the pastor is limited to people of a certain rite or nationality within certain boundaries. Such a situation arises if two or more personal parishes exist in one city and certain limits are established within which the pastors of these parishes can exclusively exercise their jurisdiction.[23]

These parishes are called mixed personal parishes because of the combined personal and territorial elements.[24] Beste distinguishes between personal and mixed parishes, limiting the term "personal" to family parishes, and the term "mixed" to national parishes.[25]

The jurisdiction which the pastor of a mixed personal parish enjoys is personal in so far as its principle of origin is a language or a nationality or a rite; and it is territorial in so far as it ex-

[23] Cf. Ciesluk, *National Parishes in the United States,* pp. 14-16.

[24] Coronata, *Institutiones Iuris Canonici,* I, n. 307; Vermeersch-Creusen, *Epitome Iuris Canonici,* I, n. 330.

[25] *Introductio in Codicem,* p. 230.

tends to the people of a particular nationality or rite who have a domicile or a quasi-domicile within the proper territorial limits of the parish. Before a person can be affiliated with a mixed personal parish, he must satisfy two requirements: he must be a member of a particular nationality or rite and at the same time have a domicile or a quasi-domicile within the parish limits.

Since, then, the jurisdiction of the pastor of a national parish is personal, he has the right and the obligation of administering Viaticum to all those within his parish boundaries who are under his jurisdiction by reason of nationality. And in so far as his jurisdiction is not strictly territorial, he has no right or obligation to administer the last sacrament to others who have a domicile or quasi-domicile within the territory of his parish, to the *peregrini* or *vagi,* or even to those who are of the same nationality as the members of the national parish, but who have not placed themselves under its jurisdiction in view of having used the option to belong to the territorial parish. The obligation of administering Holy Viaticum to these faithful would fall on the territorial pastor.

In virtue of canon 848, § 1, which states that the pastor is to administer Viaticum within his own territory even to non-parishioners, the territorial pastor has the obligation of administering the last sacrament to members of the national parish in the event that the pastor of the national parish has failed to do so. On the contrary, if the territorial pastor failed to minister the last sacrament to his own parishioners and all others subject to him within the parish limits, then the pastor of the national parish has not an equal parochial right to minister to them, since he lacks a strictly so called territorial jurisdiction over all the faithful in that territory save those who are members of his national parish.

The same principles regarding the administration of Holy Viaticum would apply with reference also to colored parishes which are not purely territorial parishes.

ARTICLE 3. RESTRICTIONS UPON THE PASTORAL RIGHT TO ADMINISTER HOLY VIATICUM

The right which the pastor has to administer Holy Viaticum is territorial. Since it is such, it can be limited by territorial restrictions.

In respect to territorial limitation, the Code itself, as it already has been noted, restricts the ordinary power of the pastor to administer Holy Viaticum to the limits of his proper parish. The pastor can administer the last sacrament outside of his proper parish boundaries in a case of necessity. But in this case of urgency the pastor would administer the sacrament not in virtue of his pastoral office, but because of the power granted by the Code to him and to all priests.[26]

In cases wherein the pastor would administer the last sacrament with at least the presumed permission of the local pastor or the local ordinary, the lawfulness of the administration would arise solely from the permission, and could not be construed in any way as arising from his pastoral office. So, even though the pastor has more extensive rights in respect to the administration of the sacrament of penance in that he can absolve his subjects anywhere,[27] yet the strict territorial limit placed upon him in the administration of Holy Viaticum is the same as that which is imposed for the administration of solemn baptism or of extreme unction, and for assistance at matrimony.[28] Hence Woywod (1880-1941) concluded: "As a general rule, one may lay down the principle that strictly pastoral functions are by law subject to the pastor of the place where such functions are to be performed."[29]

The pastor's right to administer Holy Viaticum to all the faithful within the parish is restricted territorially even within the confines of his parish. The following exceptions are made by the Code:

In the first instance, the administration of the last sacraments to the bishop of the diocese is reserved by canon 397, 3°, to the dignitaries and the canons of the cathedral chapter according to their order of precedence. If, however, the statutes of the chapter state otherwise, then the statutes are to be followed. The preced-

---

[26] Canon 848, § 2: Ceteri sacerdotes id possunt in casu tantum necessitatis aut de licentia saltem praesumpta eiusdem parochi vel Ordinarii.

[27] Cf. canon 881, § 2.

[28] Cf. canons 739; 938, § 2; 1095, §§ 1-2.

[29] "The Legislation of the Code on Baptism"—*The Homiletic and Pastoral Review* (New York, 1900-), XX (1920), 1042.

ence of the dignitaries and the canons is determined by canon 408. There it is decreed that, unless particular statutes or legitimate customs provide otherwise, the dignitaries shall have precedence over the canons, the senior canons over the junior, titular canons over the honorary, the honorary canons over the beneficiaries. Dignitaries or capitularies endowed with the episcopacy take precedence over all other dignitaries or canons who are only priests. Dignitaries take rank from the nobility of their dignity or according to the common law of precedence.

Since in this country diocesan consultors take the place of cathedral chapters, it seems that in virtue of canon 427 they share the right of administering the last sacraments to their residential bishop.[30]

As to the order of precedence, canon 106 should be followed, and particularly section 6 of the same canon which empowers the bishop to decide the question of precedence among his subjects with due regard to the principles of the common law, the legitimate customs of the diocese, and the offices committed to them.[31]

The first member in the order of precedence as established by the bishop should administer the last sacraments, unless the statutes of the diocesan consultors state otherwise.

Although the vicar general has the right of precedence over all the diocesan clerics, inclusive of the dignitaries and the canons of the cathedral church,[32] nevertheless he is denied the right and duty of administering the last sacraments to the bishop.[33]

Canon 514 exempts other certain classes of people from the pastor's jurisdiction. The canon reads that in every clerical re-

---

[30] Canon 427: Coetus consultorum dioecesanorum vices Capituli cathedralis, qua Episcopi senatus, supplet; quare quae canones ad gubernationem dioecesis, sive sede plena sive ea impedita aut vacante, Capitulo cathedrali tribuunt, ea de coetu quoque consultorum dioecesanorum intelligenda sunt.

[31] Cf. canon 106, 6°.

[32] Canon 370, § 1: Praesente etiam Episcopo, Vicarius Generalis publice privatimque praecedentiae ius habet super omnibus dioecesis clericis, non exclusis dignitatibus et canonicis ecclesiae cathedralis, etiam in choro et actibus capitularibus, nisi clericus charactere episcopali praefulgeat, et Vicarius Generalis eodem careat.

[33] S. C. C., *Resolutio, S. Iacobi de Venezuela et Aliorum,* 10 maii, 1931—*AAS,* XXIII (1931), 235.

ligious community the superior has the right and duty to administer, either in person or by another, Viaticum and extreme unction to the sick professed members and novices, and to others who dwell day and night in the religious house either as servants, or for the purpose of education, or as guests, or on account of ill health.[34]

Hence every clerical institute, whether exempt or not, whether papal or diocesan, has the privilege of attending to the spiritual needs of its own sick. By clerical institutes are understood those Orders and congregations in which according to the constitutions the majority of the members pertains actually or at least prospectively to the sacerdotal rank.[35]

The first class of sick exempted by this canon are the professed and the novices. Naturally enough, if any exemption is granted it should avail for them as the principal beneficiaries. The Pontifical Commission for the Authentic Interpretation of the Code interpreted canon 514, § 1, in the sense that the superiors have the right and duty of administering Viaticum and extreme unction to the professed and to the novices when they are ill even outside the religious house. However, the Commission added that the superiors in accordance with canon 848, § 2, must receive the local pastor's permission for a public administration of the sacrament of the Eucharist. No such permission is required for a private administration of the same sacrament.[36]

The *alii* who receive mention in canon 514, § 1, are divided into several groups according to the reason for which or the capacity in which they are residents of the monastery. They must actually dwell, i.e., have board and lodging in the religious house, or at least within the premises. The term "*domus religiosa*" is taken in the sense of the entire premises of the religious house (*intra septa monasterii*).[37] Accordingly a number of buildings may constitute

---

[34] Cf. canon 514, § 1.

[35] Cf. canon 488, 4°.

[36] Pontificia Commissio ad Codicis Canones authentice Interpretandas (*PCI*), 16 Iunii 1931—*AAS*, XXIII (1931), 353.

[37] Cf. Augustine, *A Commentary on Canon Law* (8 vols., Vol. III, 2. ed., St. Louis: Herder & Co., 1919), III, 141; De Meester, *Iuris Canonici et Iuris Canonico-Civilis Compendium*, II, 405-406; Coronata, *Institutiones Iuris Canonici*, I, 669-670; Kilker, *Extreme Unction*, p. 94.

a *domus religiosa*. Coronata points to the fact that the religious must actually dwell in these buildings.[38]

It is not required that these buildings be joined to the monastery in the sense of a single continuous structure (*per modum unius*). No matter how distinct they are from the monastery itself, as long as they form a part of the religious premises they are included under the term "religious house." Hence hospitals, residences for workers, guest-homes, schools, etc., are included in the exemption from the pastor's jurisdiction regarding the administration of the last sacraments. However, field houses, schools, colleges, hospitals, etc., which are built completely off the premises of the religious house cannot be included in the same exemption, although one or another religious resides there. A filial religious house in that it depends on a fully established religious house enjoys the exemption too. Finally, it does not matter whether the house is or is not subject to the pastor in other ways, for with regard to the administration of the last sacraments the exemption from the pastor's jurisdiction remains.[39]

The first group of the laity exempt from the pastor's jurisdiction are the workers who reside on the premises of the monastery. Whether they work for pay or from charity, they are still eligible for the right. Postulants are also included within this group.[40]

The second group of the laity mentioned in canon 514, § 1, are the students who not only receive their education but also lodge at the religious house. "Day-students" are not exempted from the pastor's jurisdiction; however, those who live at the school except during the vacation period are exempted.[41]

The third exempt group are the guests, not alone those who live in the religious house habitually, but even those who visit as tran-

---

[38] *Institutiones Iuris Canonici,* I, 670.

[39] Cf. Blat, *Commentarium Textus Codicis Iuris Canonici* (5 vols. in 6, Vol. II, 2. ed., Romae: Ex Typographia Pontificia in Instituto Pii IX, 1921), II, 562.

[40] Fanfani, *De Iure Religiosorum ad Normam Codicis Iuris Canonici* (2. ed., Taurini: Marietti, 1924), n. 415 (hereafter cited *De Iure Religiosorum*).

[41] Augustine, *A Commentary on Canon Law,* III, 143; Genicot-Salsmans, *Institutiones Theologiae Moralis,* II, 338.

sients. Persons who visit their religious friends with the intention of staying a full day and night also come within the scope of the right.[42] The duration of the stay on the part of the guests as postulated by the Code is expressed in the words *"diu noctuque."* Although some authors disagree,[43] most of the authors agree that the duration of time as postulated by the Code points to an actual stay for one entire day, or at least the actual entrance into the monastery with the intention of remaining one entire day.[44] Kilker noted that, just as a guest could satisfy in a private oratory the Sunday precept of hearing Mass if he was received for a day by the one who possesses the right of a private oratory,[45] so also *a pari* the one-day period could avail for the guest mentioned in canon 514, § 1.[46]

The last class that receives mention in canon 514, § 1, is that of sick persons who are cared for by religious in their own monasteries. If the religious have a hospital on the premises, then the inmates of the hospital would be under the jurisdiction of the religious superior. Augustine (1872-1943) noted that workingmen, etc., who would not otherwise come under this exemption would, however, have a share in it if they were nursed in the religious house.[47]

The second paragraph of canon 514 grants the ordinary confessor, or the confessor temporarily substituting in the absence of the ordinary confessor, the right and the duty of administering the last sacraments to nuns. In the law the word "nun" is restricted to those women religious who take solemn vows or who belong to an order in which according to rule solemn vows are

---

[42] Augustine, *op. cit.*, III, 144; Blat, *Commentarium Textus Codicis Iuris Canonici*, II, 562; Fanfani, *De Iure Religiosorum*, n. 415; Vermeersch-Creusen, *Epitome Iuris Canonici*, I, n. 632.

[43] E.g., Genicot-Salsmans state that a stay of several days is necessary—*Institutiones Theologiae Moralis*, II, 338.

[44] Vermeersch-Creusen, *Epitome Iuris Canonici*, I, n. 632; Augustine, *A Commentary on Canon Law*, III, 144; Coronata, *Institutiones Iuris Canonici*, I, 669; Kilker, *Extreme Unction*, p. 95.

[45] Cf. Coronata, *De Locis et Temporibus Sacris* (Augustae Taurinorum, 1922), n. 91.

[46] *Extreme Unction*, p. 95.

[47] *A Commentary on Canon Law*, III, 144.

taken, even though by Apostolic permission only simple profession is made, e.g., the Visitation nuns in the United States.[48]

Coronata and Kilker are of the opinion that the confessor's right to administer the last sacraments extends not only to nuns but to all persons residing within the limits of the convent.[49] They extend the privilege to servants, alumnae, guests, and to the sick who actually stay, or have entered the premises of the convent with the intention of staying, one complete day.

If several ordinary confessors have been appointed for the convent, then everyone of them has an equal right to administer the last sacraments. If the ordinary confessor or his temporary substitute is not available, then any priest called by the superioress can administer to the dying religious.[50]

Although they are not explicitly excepted in canon 850 or 462, 3°, yet all persons residing in a seminary must also be regarded as exempt from the parochial jurisdiction, and should receive the last sacraments from the rector of the seminary.[51] The term "all" includes servants, workmen, etc., who live on the seminary grounds. The right to administer the last sacraments as granted by the Code belongs to the rector in consequence of his official position. But he can freely yield the exercise of this right to some other priest at the seminary.

In virtue of the ruling contained in canon 1368, any seminary, whether major or minor, regional, interdiocesan, or diocesan, as long as it is legitimately erected, is exempted from parochial jurisdiction. However, the presiding at the administration of the sacrament of matrimony, and the hearing of confession outside of an urgent and grave cause, and in particular circumstances wherein

---

[48] Cf. Cocchi, *Commentarium in Codicem Iuris Canonici* (8 vols., Vol. IV, 3. ed., Augustae Taurinorum: Marietti, 1932), IV, n. 6; Coronata, *Institutiones Iuris Canonici,* I, 670.

[49] *De Sacramentis,* I, 593; *Extreme Unction,* p. 96.

[50] Cf. S. C. de Rel., *Instructio,* 6 febr., 1924—*AAS,* XVI (1924), 96; Coronata, *De Sacramentis,* I, 593; Kilker, *Extreme Unction,* p. 96.

[51] Canon 1368: Exemptum a jurisdictione paroeciali Seminarium esto; et pro omnibus qui in Seminario sunt, parochi officium, excepta materia matrimoniali et firmo praescripto can. 891, obeat Seminarii rector eiusve delegatus, nisi in quibusdam Seminariis fuerit aliter a Sede Apostolica constitutum.

the penitent himself freely approaches the seminary rector, are denied to the rector. The exemption which is implied in the ruling of canon 1368 extends even to those seminaries which, although erected for clerics alone, allow also some lay students to study there.

Although the canon speaks of a diocesan seminary, or one equal to a diocesan seminary, nevertheless the exemption seems to be enjoyed by seminaries in apostolic vicariates and prefectures. The seminaries which are conducted by religious for outside students would not, however, be exempted, except by special privilege, which the local ordinary could grant through the option which canon 464, § 2, vindicates for him.[52] Of course, if the seminary is located on the premises of the religious house, then the superior of the house would have the obligation of administering the last sacraments to its residents in consequence of the law as enacted in canon 514, § 1.

Villas or summer homes which serve as a residence for the seminarians when the latter are absent from the seminary share in the exemption which the law grants to the seminary itself.

Officials, professors, seminarians, workers, and guests are all considered as subjects of the seminary rector. Coronata notes that the rector of the seminary has the obligation of administering the sacraments to those who reside at the seminary habitually, as professors, workmen, etc., even when they are beyond the seminary limits, e.g., in a hospital or in a neighboring parish.[53]

But, since seminarians do not consider themselves as permanent residents of the seminary inasmuch as they expect to remain there no longer than until their ordination, they should be ministered to by the seminary rector when they are residing at the seminary, and by the local pastor when they are away from the seminary, as during a vacation. The same rule applies to guests at the seminary. Although an actual stay of one complete day is required by canon 514, § 1, before the superior of a clerical house may assume the right of administering the last sacraments to a guest, the guests of the seminary do not seem to fall under the

---

[52] Coronata, *Institutiones Iuris Canonici*, II, 299; Augustine, *A Commentary on Canon Law*, VI (3. ed., St. Louis: Herder & Co., 1931), 407.

[53] *Institutiones Iuris Canonici*, I, 300.

ruling of a one-day stay. Their mere presence at the seminary, no matter how short it may be, places them under the jurisdiction of the seminary rector. Canon 1368 does not explicitly state the need of a day's stay in a positive fashion. Canon 514, § 1, on the other hand, does explicitly set this requirement. From this it seems warranted to conclude that the guests at a seminary are exempt from the local pastor's jurisdiction even apart from a full day's stay.[54] Coronata states that the rector of the seminary also has the right of administering the last sacraments to the sisters living and working at the seminary.[55]

Although by virtue of canon 514, § 3, the administration of the last sacraments in institutes of lay religious devolves upon the local pastor, yet these institutions may be placed under a chaplain, to whom the ordinary can give full parochial powers in accordance with canon 464, § 2.[56] Institutes of lay religious include those communities the most of whose members are not priests, and also the congregations of women religious who are professed with simple vows.[57] Hence the Christian Brothers, the Brothers Hospitallers of St. John of God, and all sisters who take only simple vows would be under the jurisdiction of the local pastor or of the chaplain who is given parochial powers, which concession includes of course the right of administering the last sacraments. In most instances it seems that the pastor cares for the lay religious who either teach in his parochial school, perform social work within the confines of his parish, etc., and reside within his parish limits. For the larger houses, wherein many members reside, a chaplain with parochial powers is usually appointed to care for them. All

---

[54] Cf. Vermeersch, "De Exemptione Seminariorum," *Jus Pontificium* (Romae, 1921-1940), I-II (1921-1922), 70; Coronata, *Institutiones Iuris Canonici,* II, 300. Blat, however, requires the person to stay in the seminary for one day before the seminary rector can assume parochial jurisdiction over him.—*Commentarium Textus Codicis Iuris Canonici,* III, Pars II (Romae: Ex Typographia Pontificia in Instituto Pii IX, 1923), 309.

[55] *Institutiones Iuris Canonici,* II, 301; Augustine, *A Commentary on Canon Law,* VI, 407-408.

[56] "Potest Episcopus iusta et gravi de causa religiosas familias et pias domos, quae in paroeciae territorio sint et a iure non exemptae, a parochi cura subducere."

[57] Cf. can. 488, 5°.

religious of these institutes, together with their servants, guests and sick persons, are affected by this ruling.[58]

By virtue of canon 464, § 2, the ordinary may exempt from parochial jurisdiction such institutions as hospitals, asylums, orphanages, retreat-houses, etc., as long as they are destined for pious or charitable purposes. He may place these institutions under the care of a chaplain.[59] It should be noted that the appointment of a chaplain does not through that very fact exempt these places from the pastor's jurisdiction. The appointment of a chaplain may be made in a threefold manner.

A chaplain may be appointed to a charitable institution by way of a simple appointment. In such a case there is no express reference to an exemption from parochial jurisdiction either in diocesan decrees or in the appointment itself. Such a simple appointment with nothing thus specified as to exemption can be understood as a practical arrangement by which the chaplain can administer the last sacraments which the local pastor, under the circumstances which made necessary the appointment of a chaplain, is unable to administer conveniently. The pastor's jurisdiction over those institutions remains theoretically intact, and his strict right there remains undiminished. Yet there is an implied withdrawal in the sense that there is placed in charge a priest who is not canonically subject to him as an assistant. This simple appointment may be called the minimum degree of exemption which is warranted in virtue of canon 464, § 2.[60]

Secondly, it is possible for the ordinary to withdraw these charitable institutions completely from the jurisdiction of the local pastor by using the maximum degree of exemption to which the prescription of canon 464, § 2, lends itself. He can appoint the chaplain as a pastor *pleno iure,* and constitute the institutions as parishes. The chaplain in this case would have parochial jurisdiction over all those who reside in the institution, and could ad-

[58] Kilker, *Extreme Unction,* p. 97.

[59] Cf. Cocchi, *Commentarium in Codicem Iuris Canonici* (8 vols., Vol. III, 4. ed., Augustae Taurinorum: Marietti, 1937), III, n. 344; Augustine, *A Commentary on Canon Law,* II, 544; Blat, *Commentarium Textus Codicis Iuris Canonici,* II, 497.

[60] Cf. Drumm, *Hospital Chaplains,* pp. 88-89.

minister the last sacraments to the exclusion of the local pastor's right. As to those who are temporarily in these institutions as guests, the jurisdiction over them should be defined by diocesan regulations.

Thirdly, the ordinary can simply appoint the chaplain with full pastoral power. In this case the chaplain would not be a pastor exercising the pastoral functions in his own name, but as a delegate with full powers. Such a simple appointment would not entail full pastoral jurisdiction, and hence the chaplain should possess definite proof of such a grant of jurisdiction in his document of appointment.[61] Though the chaplain's pastoral jurisdiction would come to him when he is appointed to his office as chaplain, yet it would be a delegated and not an ordinary jurisdiction. Ordinary jurisdiction is attached to an office *ipso iure,* while the jurisdiction which would come to him in this instance would derive not *a iure,* but *ab homine.* Such a chaplain, therefore, would act as a delegate of the ordinary; he could be removed at will; his rights could be curtailed or withdrawn by a simple revocation. He could administer the last sacraments with as equal jurisdiction as the minister having jurisdiction *a iure.*[62]

In regard to hospital chaplains Drumm states that without doubt the most common method by which the local ordinaries take care of the spiritual needs of large Catholic hospitals is by the appointment of chaplains for them without any express reference to exemption from parochial jurisdiction, either in the diocesan decrees or in the appointment itself.[63]

Drumm points out that the right obtained by simple appointment to administer the last sacraments to patients in hospitals is based more on moral rather than on canonical arguments. He states:

> From the negative point of view, in consideration of the nature of a hospital as a place serving exclusively

[61] Canon 200, § 2: Ei qui delegatum se asserit, incumbit onus probandae delegationis.

[62] Cf. Waldron, *The Minister of Baptism,* The Catholic University of America Canon Law Studies, n. 170 (Washington, D. C.: The Catholic University of America Press, 1942), pp. 114-115.

[63] Drumm, *Hospital Chaplains,* p. 97.

> the sick, if the appointment of a chaplain did not imply some right and duty to administer the last sacraments, the chief purpose of the appointment would be frustrated. Conceivably a hospital chaplain may not have the right to administer the anointing [or Holy Viaticum], although that would be an exceptional case. As a general rule, this right is associated with a hospital chaplaincy. As Fanfani states, "from Apostolic privilege, from custom, or the disposition of the local ordinary, almost everywhere there is induced a quasi-parochial status for the hospital chaplains as regards the last sacraments."[64]
>
> Although the hospital chaplain only simply appointed is considered here without reference to any higher status given him by Apostolic privilege or custom or the expressed disposition of the latter, it can be safely asserted that in general he has the right to administer these sacraments. The reason for this is the close nexus almost universally recognized between the administration of the last sacraments and the functions of hospital chaplains.[65]

Concerning the relationship between the hospital chaplain and the pastors of national parishes, it can be said that canon 464, § 2, in virtue of which the hospital chaplain receives his jurisdiction, and in which mention is made of pious houses which are in the territory of a parish—*quae in paroeciae territorio sint*—refers primarily to territorial pastors. Hence, since any withdrawal from the jurisdiction of the pastor must be strictly interpreted, it seems that even exemption by the formal decree of the local ordinary without qualification would refer only to the exemption from the jurisdiction of the local parish, and not necessarily from that of the language parish. To know whether or not the hospital chaplain can under ordinary circumstances administer the last sacraments to members of a national parish, the bishop in establishing the chaplaincy should explicitly express his intention. If he has not done so, then the particular circumstances surrounding the exemption, or the fact that all parishes in the vicinity are language parishes, could determine the status of the hospital chaplain in relationship to the patients of these "nationals."[66]

[64] *De Iure Parochorum,* n. 480.

[65] Drumm, *Hospital Chaplains,* p. 93.

[66] Cf. Drumm, *op. cit.,* p. 99.

The principles enunciated above for parishioners of national parishes are applicable also to patients who pertain to different rites.

The pastor's right and obligation to administer Holy Viaticum as well as extreme unction can be lost personally through the incurring of penalties. Hence a pastor can be forced to surrender his right to the administration of the last sacraments, if he has incurred an excommunication,[67] a suspension *a divinis*,[68] or a personal interdict.[69]

In the first place, if the pastor has incurred a *latae sententiae* penalty, which fact has not as yet been certified by means of a declaratory sentence, and the crime is at the same time not notorious, then he is not bound to observe the penalty in the external forum if such an observance would result in danger of scandal or in the loss of his good name.[70] Such a pastor, though bound by the penalty in the internal forum, would frequently find it necessary to administer the last sacraments even when there was not a case of urgent necessity, since a refusal to do so would excite untoward astonishment in the minds of the parishioners. In such cases he would act not only validly but also licitly.

A pastor who is excommunicated simply, or suspended, or personally interdicted apart from any declaratory or condemnatory sentence, even though his crime be notorious, can validly and licitly administer the sacraments as often as the faithful legitimately seek them from him. The pastor in such circumstances is not obliged to inquire into the reasons of the one desiring to receive the sacraments.[71] It appears that under these circumstances the pastor could even show himself ready to administer the sacraments, in such a manner that the people could easily approach him.

---

[67] Cf. canons 2257 and 2261, §§ 1-3.

[68] Cf. canons 2278 and 2279, § 2, 2°—"A pastor suspended *a iurisdictione*, while he may not administer ecclesiastical property nor hear confessions, because these acts entail jurisdiction, may nevertheless baptize and administer Holy Viaticum and Extreme Unction."—Rainer, *Suspension of Clerics*, p. 79.

[69] Cf. canons 2268 and 2275, 2°.

[70] Cf. canon 2232, § 1; Conran, *The Interdict*, The Catholic University of America Canon Law Studies, n. 56 (Washington, D. C.: The Catholic University of America, 1930), pp. 51-55.

[71] Cf. canons 2261, § 2; 2275, 2°; 2284.

Furthermore, the petition of the faithful need not be explicit. Even an implicit or reasonably presumed request would suffice, such as would obtain if the good of souls demanded such an administration and there were no other priests present.[72]

However, priests who are *excommunicati vitandi,* or who are excommunicated or suspended or personally interdicted upon the passing of a condemnatory or a declaratory sentence can administer the last sacraments to only those who are in urgent need of them, and even then they may do so only when there is no other priest present. As has been noted, the confession of a person who is in danger of death can be heard by any censured priest, even if other priests are present for the hearing of the confession.[73]

It must be remembered that the lawfulness of the administration of the last sacrament under the above mentioned circumstances is assured solely from the viewpoint of the Church's requirements in its penal legislation. If the censured priest were simultaneously in a state of mortal sin, his administration of the last sacraments as sanctioned in the Church's penal legislation would of course not be unlawful, but it would be illicit by reason of the unrepented sin which burdens his conscience.[74]

If a pastor would temporarily disregard his suspension, interdict, or excommunication, and administer the last sacraments under the circumstances which the Code prescribes for his lawful administration of the sacraments, the pastor would not be violating the inflicted penalty. By force of the law itself he regains the use of his Orders. Thus, if he administers the sacraments while he is under these penalties, either to protect his good name and reputation,[75] or because the faithful legitimately petition their administration,[76] there is no actual violation of the inflicted penalty, and consequently no irregularity is incurred.[77]

---

[72] Cf. Waldron, *The Minister of Baptism,* pp. 103-105; Rainer, *The Suspension of Clerics,* pp. 84-85; and Conran, *The Interdict,* p. 97.

[73] Cf. canons 2261, § 3; 2275, 2°; 2284; 882.

[74] Cerato, *Censurae Vigentes Ipso Facto a Codice Iuris Canonici Excerptae,* n. 37; Sole, *De Delictis et Poenis* (Romae, 1920), n. 220.

[75] Canon 2232, § 1.

[76] Canon 2261, §§ 2-3.

[77] Canon 985, 7°; cf. Rainer, *Suspension of Clerics,* p. 190.

ARTICLE 4. OTHER LICIT MINISTERS

> Canon 848, § 2: Ceteri sacerdotes id possunt in casu tantum necessitatis aut de licentia saltem praesumpta eiusdem parochi vel Ordinarii.

In a case of necessity, which need not be extreme, any priest may lawfully administer Holy Viaticum. The necessary faculty for the licit distribution of this sacrament in such circumstances is obtained from the Code itself. The necessity can be physical or moral. The former arises when the proper minister cannot possibly reach the sick person. The latter arises when he cannot be called or when he cannot administer it without most serious inconvenience. The necessity for another minister than the proper one can be occasioned either on the side of the proper minister or on the side of the stricken person.

On the side of the proper minister a physical necessity for another priest's administration of the last sacrament would be constituted if the proper minister could not possibly reach the stricken person, either because of illness, or because of too great a distance from the stricken person, or because of the multiplied number of other stricken persons who require his care. On the side of the proper minister a moral necessity would arise for another priest's administration of the last sacrament if the proper minister has refused or declined his service, if he is in a state of mortal sin, or if he is excommunicated, suspended or personally interdicted. On the side of the stricken person there would arise a physical necessity for the administration by some priest other than the proper minister if the person were in such danger of death that to wait for the proper minister would make it impossible for the dying person to receive Holy Viaticum. On the side of the stricken person there would result a moral necessity for his reception of the sacrament at the hands of any priest if the desire for spiritual help, specifically by receiving Holy Viaticum, would be so ardent and great that only an administration by the first available priest would furnish the help that is so ardently sought.[78]

nata, *De Sacramentis,* I, 278.

---

[78] Jorio, *La Comunione agl' Infermi* (Romae: Pustet, 1931), n. 84; Coro-

If the pastor unreasonably refuses to administer the last sacrament and likewise fails to give permission to another, then a moral necessity arises, and in such a case the priest may proceed with a safe conscience, since he can reasonably presume permission on the part of the local ordinary.[79] Such a priest is then constituted by the law itself as the extraordinary minister of the sacrament.[80]

Since the pastor is the ordinary minister of Viaticum, he may authorize any other priest to administer this sacrament.[81] The ordinary of the place where the stricken person is present can also grant permission. Such permission cannot be nullified through any contrary wish of the pastor. The very fact that the ordinary can grant this permission evinces his possession of the personal right to administer the sacrament within his own territory. The committing of a power presupposes the possession of that same power by the committing agent.

Although curates supply the pastor's place in the parochial ministry, nevertheless the pastor can reserve this function to himself with the result that any administration by the curate against the pastor's will would be unlawful.[82] If the faculties or diocesan statutes give curates the right of administration, then they can bestow the sacrament licitly even against the will of the pastor. In such a case they have the ordinary's permission.[83] If the authorization given to the curate includes all sick-calls, then the latter may in turn authorize another priest for individual sick-calls.[84]

Since any priest may administer in a case of necessity, the permission may be granted to any priest. However, an excommunicated, suspended, or a personally interdicted priest should administer the sacrament in a case of necessity only under the conditions

---

[79] Vermeersch-Creusen, *Epitome Iuris Canonici,* II, 114, 2.

[80] Blat, *Commentarium Textus Codicis Iuris Canonici,* Vol. III, pars I (Romae: Ex Typographia Pontificia in Instituto Pii IX, 1923), 180; 341.

[81] Canon 199, § 1.

[82] Cf. canons 476, § 6, and 462, § 3; Bastnagel, "Parish Assistants and the Prenuptial Investigation," *The Jurist* (Washington, D. C., 1941-), VII (1947), 171-174.

[83] Cf. Augustine, *A Commentary on Canon Law,* IV (2. ed., St. Louis: Herder & Co., 1920), 399.

[84] Canon 199, § 3.

and circumstances which make the administration allowable for such a penalized priest.[85] Such a priest is not ordinarily desirable as one to whom the permission may be granted, and he should be given permission only when more worthy priests are not available.

The permission may be given explicitly, i.e., in writing, orally, or by signs, or implicitly, i.e., through acts which in their circumstances reasonably reflect a grant of permission. It may also be legitimately presumed, e.g., when it is foreseen that it would be readily granted, or that the pastor would be pleased if he were spared the personal inconvenience of a personal administration. This presumption could obtain even when there is no canonical reason present for the granting of the permission, but then a more intimate knowledge of the pastor personally is undoubtedly required if such a presumption is to stand as duly warranted.

Under all these cases a priest becomes the lawful extraordinary minister of the sacrament. A priest who administers Holy Viaticum in any other case commits a grievous sin, because he invades the right of the pastor in a matter of important concern.

Since the deacon is the extraordinary minister of Holy Communion in virtue of the Order of diaconate, he may distribute Holy Communion under the circumstances postulated in the Code. A grave reason must be present for the distribution, and the permission of the local ordinary or the pastor must be had. Permission may be presumed in a case of necessity.[86]

The deacon could certainly administer Viaticum licitly to a person in danger of death. Such a case would constitute a grave cause for the administration of the sacrament. However, the following conditions would have to be fulfilled, namely, that neither the proper minister nor another priest be available, and that the requisite permission of the local pastor or of the ordinary be previously obtained. In a case of necessity the deacon could legitimately presume permission.[87]

---

[85] Cf. *supra*, pp. 82-83.

[86] Cf. canon 845, § 2.

[87] Jorio, *La Comunione agl' Infermi*, n. 85; Augustine, *A Commentary on Canon Law*, IV, 214; Piscetta-Gennaro, *Elementa Theologiae Moralis*, V, 521; Noldin-Schmitt, *Summa Theologiae Moralis*, III, 126-127; Gasparri, *De Sanctissima Eucharistia* (2 vols., Parisiis et Lugduni, 1897), II, 1079;

A deacon who would outside of a case of necessity minister Holy Viaticum without the proper permission would sin grievously, because he would be violating an ecclesiastical law of serious moment.[88] Some authors are of the opinion that a deacon would not sin grievously by administering Holy Viaticum without the proper permission as long as his act did not evince any contempt of the law, and at the same time definitely did not offer any occasion for the emergence of scandal.[89]

Although it is disputed whether or not a deacon who administers Holy Viaticum illicitly incurs thereby an irregularity,[90] the opinion which denies the contracting of the irregularity seems the more probable one to the writer. Through his reception of the Order of diaconate the deacon receives the faculty of administering Holy Communion in a secondary, auxiliary, or supplementary capacity. Consequently it appears that the deacon does not incur an irregularity, for he simply exercises the function of an Order which he legitimately possesses by ordination. Cappello states that an illicit administration of Holy Communion connotes an infringement upon jurisdictional rights rather than a usurpation of the functions of an Order.[91]

Concerning the administration of Holy Viaticum by minor clerics and lay persons, most of the authors admit that under certain circumstances these may licitly act as ministers for a person who is in danger of death.[92] The following reasons are given for this opinion:

Coronata, *De Sacramentis,* I, 270-271; Prümmer, *Manuale Theologiae Moralis* (3. ed., 3 vols., Friburgi Brisgoviae, 1923), III, n. 217; Cappello, *De Sacramentis,* I, 269.

[88] Coronata, *De Sacramentis,* I, 272; Prümmer, *op. cit.,* III, n. 217; Cappello, *op. cit.,* I, 268-269.

[89] Coronata, *De Sacramentis,* I, 272; Cappello, *op. cit.,* I, 268-269.

[90] Cf. canon 985, 7°.

[91] Cappello, *De Sacramentis,* I, 269; Coronata, *De Sacramentis,* I, 272; Gasparri, *De Sacra Ordinatione* (2 vols., Parisiis, 1893), I, n. 341; Regatillo, *Ius Sacramentarium* (2 vols., Santander: Sal Terrae, 1945-1946), I, 169.

[92] Suarez, *Opera Omnia* (28 vols., Parisiis, 1856-1861), Disp. LXII, sect. I, n. 10—XXI, 579; Laymann, *Theologia Moralis,* Lib. V, tract. 4, cap. 7, n. 5—p. 329; St. Alphonsus, *Theologia Moralis,* Lib. VI, n. 237—Vol. II, 197-198; Noldin-Schmitt, *Summa Theologiae Moralis,* III, 125; Augus-

1. The obligation of receiving Holy Viaticum derives from the divine law itself. But certainly the divine law which commands the reception of Holy Viaticum prevails over the ecclesiastical law which prescribes the manner in which and the minister by whom the sacrament is to be administered.

2. The administration of Viaticum by minor clerics or by lay people would be prohibited either because of the irreverence resulting from the laity's touching of the Sacred Species, or because of the impropriety inherent in their ministering or distributing the sacrament, or because of their debarment by either the divine or the ecclesiastical law. The lay administration of Viaticum is not prohibited for the first of these reasons, for history shows that the faithful in the early centuries were wont to receive the Holy Eucharist with their own hands. Secondly, the ministering and the distributing of the sacrament in a case of urgent necessity would not be an act of impropriety if undertaken by minor clerics or by lay people, for the proper dispositions are postulated on the part of the stricken person, and due reverence is prerequired in the actions of the minor cleric or of the lay person who administers Holy Viaticum. Thirdly, neither the divine law nor the ecclesiastical law sets any debarment to lay administration in cases of urgent necessity.

3. It cannot be argued that lay administration of Viaticum is contrary to the universal custom of the Church, for the early history of the Church gives evidence that the lay people carried Communion to the sick, and that this custom prevailed until the tenth century.

4. Any scandal which might result from lay administration could readily be obviated by means of a proper instruction of the faithful. It could be made clear to the laity that in any emergency wherein they would be called on to administer the sacrament they would be obliged to do so with the greatest reverence, and it also could be explained to the bystanders either before or after that

---

tine, *A Commentary on Canon Law,* IV, 514; Cappello, *De Sacramentis,* I, 270; Gasparri, *De Sanctissima Eucharistia,* II, 1080; Coronata, *De Sacramentis,* I, 271.

the unusual circumstances warranted for lay people their administration of the Holy Eucharist by way of Holy Viaticum.

5. The Holy See itself permitted the Mexican as well as the Russian ordinaries to allow a lay administration in their countries during the recent persecutions.[93]

Before minor clerics or devout lay persons may licitly administer the last sacrament, there must be an urgent need for its administration. The stricken person must be in danger of death. Furthermore, they can administer Holy Viaticum in only such circumstances in which neither a priest nor a deacon is available, and when the permission of the local pastor or of the local ordinary has been obtained or can reasonably be presumed as given. Of course, if the person is so near to death that there remains no time to seek the proper permission, then they may licitly administer the Holy Viaticum on a presumed permission. This usually would be the circumstance under which the laity would minister.

In circumstances wherein a general need for lay administration is foreseen, an explicit mandate should be given by the local ordinary, e.g., during a persecution, or a pestilence, or a war. Jorio states that in cases of general necessity the local ordinary should first seek the advice of the Holy See before granting a general permission. If the circumstances are such that no time avails for the seeking of this advice, then the bishop could grant permission to his faithful, instructing them of course to administer the Holy Eucharist only in urgent necessity with great reverence and with

---

[93] S. C. de Sacr., Private Reply, March 22, 1927—Bouscaren, *Canon Law Digest* (2 vols., Milwaukee: Bruce, 1934, 1943), II, 28; Bouscaren also mentions that an indult was granted to Russia on January 20, 1930, through which the ordinaries in Russia were empowered to permit pious laymen to carry Holy Communion to Catholics in prison, etc.,—*op. cit.,* II, 207. St. Thomas and other theologians maintained that lay administration was contrary to the universal practice of the Church, and that, since the reception of Viaticum was not indispensably necessary as a means of salvation, its extraordinary administration by minor clerics or by lay people was unlawful. —*Sancti Thomae Aquinatis Commentum in Quatuor Libros Sententiarum* (2 vols., Parmae, 1858), Lib. IV, dist. 13, q. 1, art. 3, sol. 1-3—Vol. II, 675; De Lugo, *Disputationes Scholasticae et Morales, Tractatus de Sacramento Eucharistiae,* Disp. XVIII, sect. 1, n. 22—Vol. IV, 173.

the proper obviation of all likely scandal. In the meantime recourse should be made to the Holy See.[94]

Recent authors maintain that a priest may administer Holy Viaticum to himself if another priest is not present to administer It.[95] Although Coronata and Cappello claim that a priest should minister Holy Communion to himself even when a deacon is present,[96] nevertheless, when the priest is seriously ill or near danger of nevertheless, when the priest is seriously ill or near danger of death, the deacon could assist him and minister to him.[97] The deacon should minister Viaticum to himself only when a priest or some other deacon is unavailable.

Recent authors likewise maintain that minor clerics and lay people probably can give Viaticum to themselves when a priest or a deacon is unavailable. The lay person should be ministered to by a minor cleric rather than by another lay person whenever this is possible. When neither a priest, nor a deacon, nor a minor cleric is at hand for the administration, and particularly when the person has had no opportunity to confess or to be anointed, he may administer the last sacrament to himself.[98] Cappello claims that this probable opinion may be accepted as a certain doctrine, particularly if the self-communicants are careful to preclude all scandal and irreverence.[99] He bases this opinion on the fact that this practice was common in the early days of the Church during the persecutions, and that the Holy See declared it a licit practice in individual instances.[100]

---

[94] *La Comunione agl' Infermi,* nn. 94-98.

[95] Gasparri, *De Sanctissima Eucharistia,* II, 1081; Augustine, *A Commentary on Canon Law,* IV, 215; Piscetta-Gennaro, *Elementa Theologiae Moralis,* V, 523; Cappello, *De Sacramentis,* I, 269; Prümmer, *Manuale Theologiae Moralis,* III, n. 218; Aertnys-Damen, *Theologia Moralis* (13. ed., 2 vols., Taurini-Romae: Marietti, 1939), II, n. 122.

[96] *De Sacramentis,* I, 272; *De Sacramentis,* I, 269.

[97] Cf. canon 845, § 2.

[98] Cf. Coronata, *De Sacramentis,* I, 273; Prümmer, *Manuale Theologiae Moralis,* III, n. 218; Piscetta-Gennaro, *Elementa Theologiae Moralis,* V, 523; Gasparri, *De Sanctissima Eucharistia,* II, 1081; Noldin-Schmitt, *Summa Theologiae Moralis,* III, 127.

[99] *De Sacramentis,* I, 273-274.

[100] E.g., S. C. de Prop. Fide (C. P. pro Sin.—*Tunkin. Occident.*), 21 iul. 1841: "An permitti potest in hoc persecutionis tempore ut fidei confessores

Self-administration of Holy Viaticum is expected to be a very rare need. A priest who while stationed in an outlying district is stricken rather suddenly, and who cannot call upon any priest or deacon to assist him, can licitly administer the last sacrament to himself. In emergencies, e.g., during pestilences, persecutions, wars, etc., in view of the lack of priests, either because many have been killed or because the remaining ones have too great a number of emergency cases to care for, the laity could in the absence of deacons or minor clerics minister the Holy Eucharist to one another.

Minor clerics and the laity would sin grievously by illicitly administering Viaticum to one another, and furthermore they would incur an irregularity.[101]

ARTICLE 5. PUBLIC AND PRIVATE ADMINISTRATION OF HOLY VIATICUM

There is a public and a private administration of Holy Viaticum. The administration of Holy Communion to the sick and to those who are in danger of death is public when the rites and ceremonies prescribed by the Roman Ritual for a public administration are carried out.[102] Holy Communion should be brought to the sick publicly; however, a just and reasonable cause may make a private administration advisable. Authors agree that the just and reasonable cause need not be a grave one. The following are some of the causes considered as reasonably justifying a private administration:

1. Avoidance of the danger of irreverence, particularly in those family in whose residence the stricken person is present conducts

---

ad mortem propter fidem damnati, et quibus in carcere defertur SS. Eucharistiae Sacramentum occulte, possint illud suis manibus accipere et sese occulte communicare, ne sacerdos illos more ordinario communicans a persecutoribus agnoscatur et prehendatur; vel satiusne est in illo casu ab illis confessoribus communicandis abstinere, maximo cum illorum animae detrimento?" Affirmative quoad primam partem, dummodo nullo irreverentiae aut conculcationis periculo tantum Sacramentum exponatur."

[101] Cf. canon 985, 7°.

[102] Cf. Cappello, *De Sacramentis,* I, 357; *Rituale Romanum* (New York: Benziger Brothers, Inc., 1944), Tit. IV, cap. 4, *De Communione Infirmorum,* nn. 1028.

territories where many unbelievers and heretics live. Coronata states that even in these territories Viaticum should be administered publicly to patients in Catholic institutions such as asylums, hospitals, etc., where Catholics alone are received, or where non-Catholics indeed are received but at the same time are subject to a full Catholic routine.[103]

2. Reasonable opposition of the people to a public administration of Holy Viaticum or Holy Communion. If, for example, the a business and sincerely believes that its business would suffer after non-Catholic clients witness the priest administering the last sacrament in a public manner, the priest would be justified under such circumstances to administer privately.

3. Cases of urgent necessity which imply serious difficulty for the public administration of the sacrament of the Eucharist. The necessity may arise either on the part of the minister or on the part of the stricken person. A great inconvenience encountered by the priest in having too many public administrations of Viaticum at one time would be a sufficient cause for Its private administration.[104]

In the United States the II Plenary Council of Baltimore in 1866 decreed that the Blessed Sacrament should be carried to the sick privately. It was a general prescript for the entire country, and remains in effect to the present day.[105]

There was question regarding who had the right to decide whether or not a just and reasonable cause exists for the licit private administration of this last sacrament. Before the decree of the Sacred Congregation of the Sacraments in 1928 most of the canonists were of the opinion that the judge regarding the private or public carrying of Holy Communion was the priest him-

---

[103] *De Sacramentis,* I, 277.

[104] Coronata, *De Sacramentis,* I, 277; Cappello, *De Sacramentis,* I, 356; Vermeersch-Creusen, *Epitome Iuris Canonici,* II, n. 114, 1.

[105] *Concilii Plenarii Baltimorensis II Acta et Decreta* (Baltimorae: John Murphy, 1868), Tit. IV, cap. 4, *De Sanctissimo Eucharistiae Sacramento,* n. 264, pp. 142-143; Woywod, *A Practical Commentary on the Code of Canon Law* (2 vols., Tenth Printing, New York: Joseph F. Wagner, 1946), I, 404-405.

self.[106] Then the Sacred Congregation of the Sacraments in a reply to the bishops of Spain declared that the sole judge is the local ordinary.[107]

However, the Congregation added that if according to common experience and judgment there exists in the diocese, or in any particular place, no objection against the bringing of Holy Communion privately to the sick, then ordinaries must be on their guard lest by rules which are too rigorous or too comprehensive in requiring that Holy Communion be brought publicly, or by a reservation to themselves of the faculty of granting permission for the bringing of Holy Communion privately in individual cases, they withhold from the sick the opportunity of receiving Communion even daily.

But this did not seem to solve the question, for even after the Congregation's declaration some authors still maintained that in individual cases the priest is the judge of whether a just and reasonable cause is present for a private administration.[108] Vidal (1868-1939) stated that with regard to an introduction of the general practice of private administration the judge of the justifying cause or causes that warrant such a general practice is solely the local ordinary. However, he claimed that since canon 849, § 1,[109] treated of the sick in a particular case, regardless of whether in a particular territory there existed the practice of a private or a public administration, the ministering priest is the judge of the existing cause that warrants a private administration. He based his solution on the statement: *"Silente lege, ad eum pertinet iudicare de verificato casu (de existentia iustae causae), cui pro tali casu datur in iure potestas ponendi actum, alia ratione non limitata."*[110]

---

[106] Cf. Vermeersch-Creusen, *Epitome Iuris Canonici,* II (2. ed., Bruxellis et Brugis, 1925), n. 636; Regatillo, *Ius Sacramentarium,* I, 170.

[107] S. C. de Sacr., *Romana et Aliarum,* 5 ian. 1928—*AAS,* XX (1928), 81.

[108] Jorio, *La Comunione agl' Infermi,* n. 111; Wernz-Vidal, *Ius Canonicum ad Codicis Normam Exactum* (7 vols. in 8, Vol. IV, Pars I, Romae: Apud Aedes Universitatis Gregorianae, 1934), IV, pars I, 146-147 (hereafter cited as *Ius Canonicum*); Cappello, *De Sacramentis,* I, 355-356; Regatillo, *Ius Sacramentarium,* I, 170-172.

[109] "Communionem privatim ad infirmos quilibet sacerdos deferre potest, de venia saltem praesumpta sacerdotis, cui custodia sanctissimi Sacramenti commissa est."

[110] *Ius Canonicum,* IV, pars I, 146-147.

Certainly in particular sick calls the local ordinary cannot possibly be the judge of the cause, simply for the reason that he is not present there to judge. Vidal's solution seems to be a convincing one.[111]

ARTICLE 6. THE RITES AND CEREMONIES OF PUBLIC AND PRIVATE ADMINISTRATION

For the public administration the rites and ceremonies as prescribed by the *Roman Ritual* for the public administration are to be followed.[112] In the private administration the rites and ceremonies as prescribed by the *Roman Ritual* for the private administration are to be followed.[113]

---

[111] Cappello states that in principle (*per se*) the priest does not need permission from the local ordinary to administer the Eucharist privately to the sick. He insists that the faculty is granted by the Code to the priest, and cannot be restricted by an inferior prelate. Nor, properly considered, so Cappello maintains, can the ordinary in principle (*per se*) be the sole judge of a just and reasonable cause, since the Code states nothing of this power of the ordinary, and furthermore in some instances the ordinary cannot possibly be the judge. Cappello states that the local ordinary cannot prohibit the private administration by synodal laws or general precepts, since the private administration is granted and permitted by the Code itself. Nor can the local ordinary reserve by law or general precept the judgment regarding the existence of a just and reasonable cause, and consequently the right of granting permissions in individual cases for the private administration. On the contrary, the ordinary may forbid the private administration in this or in that parish or section of the diocese; he may forbid the private administration at Easter-tide or at another time; or he may reserve to himself by particular precept the faculty of granting permission for the private administration in a particular case, v.g., for this or that priest, or under certain determined circumstances, or for a certain stricken person. The ordinary may legitimately do these things, because it is his duty and right to urge the observance of the ecclesiastical laws, to see that no abuses of ecclesiastical discipline creep in, and, if they are present, to check them prudently by opportune advice and precepts to which even the exempt religious are subject. —*De Sacramentis*, I, 355-356.

[112] Tit. IV, cap. 4, *De Communione Infirmorum*, nn. 6-28.

[113] Tit. IV, cap. 4, *De Communione Infirmorum*, n. 29.—Quando ex iusta et rationabili causa privatim sacra communio ad infirmos defertur, Sacerdos saltem stolam semper habeat propriis coopertam vestibus; in sacculo seu bursa pyxidem recondat, quam per funiculos collo appensam in sinu reponat;

In the United States, it may be safely said, two of the prescripts are not universally carried out, namely, that a cleric or at least a layman accompany the ministering priest, and that the cassock and the surplice be worn by the priest in the sickroom of the stricken person. Must it be said that such discrepancies with the prescripts of the *Roman Ritual* are outright violations of liturgical law, or have perhaps legitimate customs been established contrary to these prescripts?

If one denies the fact that a custom can legitimately be established contrary to liturgical law, then of course one would have to conclude without any further discussion that the two current practices in this country are outright violations of liturgical law.

Granted, however, that a custom can legitimately be established as contrary to liturgical law, as many authors believe,[114] then one must see whether these two practices can be accepted as reasonable, in consequence of which they may then be regarded as legitimately established customs contrary to the prescripts of the *Roman Ritual.* It must be kept in mind that, although the authors maintain that a custom can be established contrary to liturgical laws, nevertheless practically everyone admits that the Church, in an attempt to maintain unity in its authentically approved rites and ceremonies, very seldom acknowledges a custom contrary to these rites and ceremonies as reasonable, and in fact usually disavows all toleration of it.

It appears, first of all, that if these two customs were established before the II Plenary Council of Baltimore, then they were abrogated by the Council. The Council decreed that the Holy Eucharist was to be administered privately in this country because of the prevailing adverse circumstances of those times. However, the Council specifically decreed that the prescripts of the *Roman*

---

et numquam solus procedat, sed uno saltem fideli, in defectu clerici, associetur. Cum autem ad infirmi cubiculum pervenerit, Sacerdos superpelliceum quoque induat cum stola, si illud antea non induerit.

[114] De Meester, *Iuris Canonici et Iuris Canonico-Civilis Compendium,* I, 189-190; Vermeersch-Creusen, *Epitome Iuris Canonici,* I, n. 143; Beste, *Introductio in Codicem,* p. 100; Guilfoyle, *Custom,* The Catholic University of America Canon Law Studies, n. 105 (Washington, D. C.: The Catholic University of America, 1937), pp. 121-122.

Ritual should be observed most diligently in so far as circumstances permitted.[115] The Council explicitly mentioned the necessity of using a pyx, stole, surplice and cassock. This particular conciliar decree was a special law enacted for the United States, and thus it abrogated the extant contrary customs. According to the pre-Code legislation, similarly as the law obtains now, a plenary council had such power of abrogation. Perchance a supposition may be made that the practices were immemorial customs at the time of the II Plenary Council. Would the Council have abrogated such immemorial customs by that particular decree? Pre-Code canonists inferred that an immemorial custom was not abrogated unless: (a) the law declared that all contrary customs were abolished; (b) a reason was expressed in the law against an immemorial custom; (c) the law abrogated every custom, even those which it left undesignated.[116]

In this particular decree, it seems evident that the Council urged the priests to supply for the absence of the pomp of a public administration by means of an internal devotion, and at the same time to exercise, to the best of their power, an externally manifest reverence for the Blessed Sacrament.[117]

Certainly the exhortation to the exercise of an externally manifest reverence connoted a cogent enough reason for the discon-

---

[115] *Concilii Plenarii Baltimorensis II Acta et Decreta,* Tit. V, cap. 4, *De Sanctissimo Eucharistiae Sacramento,* n. 264, pp. 142-143: "Dolendum sane est rerum adjuncta, quae apud nos obtinent, impedire quominus ea cum pompa, quam vult Ecclesia, ad infirmos deferatur Sanctissimum Sacramentum. . . . Quaenam vero sit urgens causa, ex loci, temporis, aliisque adjunctis erit dijudicandum. Injungimus 'presbyteris strictam obligationem semper in hisce casibus Sanctam Hostiam super pectus deferendi.' Numquam, nisi in extrema necessitate vel ipsam Hostiam, vel vas sacrum in quo servatur, stola saltem non induti attrectent. Cum in ecclesia Sanctissimum e tabernaculo extrahunt, semper superpelliceo et stola sint induti. Infirmis Sacram Eucharistiam ministrantes, praescripta Ritualis Romani, in quantum rerum circumstantiae sinunt, diligentissime servent."

[116] Guilfoyle, *Custom,* pp. 67-68.

[117] *Concilii Plenarii Baltimorensis II Acta et Decreta,* Tit. V, cap. 4, *De Sanctissimo Eucharistiae Sacramento,* n. 264, p. 142: "Studeant itaque sacerdotes, ut interno animi devotione hujus pompae defectum suppleant, simulque haud negligant quantum in ipsis est reverentiae externae, quae Christo revera praesenti debetur, prospicere."

tinuance of any custom which abstracted from another person's accompaniment of the priest on the sick-call, and from the priest's wearing of the proper vestments in the sick-room. Hence it seems evident that the II Plenary Council of Baltimore abrogated even contrary immemorial customs if any of the contrary customs had existed for that long period of time.

The Holy See itself looked unfavorably on the practice of not wearing a cassock, a surplice, and a stole. In a private reply in the year 1826 the Sacred Congregation of Rites rejected the custom, practiced in a certain diocese, of carrying the Blessed Sacrament for a long distance in the outlying country districts without the proper vestments. The Sacred Congregation insisted that the custom be eliminated.[118] In a later reply to a vicariate apostolic the Sacred Congregation of Rites declared that, although it would be licit to carry the Blessed Sacrament without the sacred vestments and candles to the sick and the incarcerated in territories where there is danger of the commission of sacrilege by the infidels and heretics, nevertheless the wearing of the cassock and of the stole in the room of the sick person or the incarcerated one should not be omitted. These vestments were to be worn whenever it was possible to do so.[119] Although these private responses of the Sacred Congregation had no legal effect on the practice in the United States, yet they indicate how unfavorably the Holy See viewed the practice of not wearing the proper vestments in the sick-room.

Furthermore, if the two customs gained currency anew after the Council of Baltimore had abrogated them, then notwithstanding their second establishment they were abrogated by the law promulgated in the present Code, since neither of the customs could be centenary or immemorial at the time when the present Code became the binding law in 1918.[120]

---

[118] S. C. R., *Gandaven.*, 16 dec. 1826—*Decreta Authentica Congregationis Sacrorum Rituum ex Actis eiusdem Collecta eiusque Auctoritate Promulgata sub Auspiciis SS. D. N. Leonis Papae XIII* (5 vols. et 2 Appendices, Romae. Typis Polyglottis Vaticanis, 1898-1927), n. 2650 (hereafter cited as *Decr. Auth.*).

[119] S. C. R., *Vicariatus Apostolici de Dania*, 4 febr. 1871—*Decr. Auth.*, n. 3234.

[120] Canon 5: Vigentes in praesens contra horum statuta canonum consuetudines sive universales sive particulares, si quidem ipsis canonibus expresse

There now needs to be considered the further question whether these practices, if again they became current after the enactment of the Code, may be considered as reasonable enough under the present circumstances to permit their existence. In the light of the present circumstances the practice of the priest's not being accompanied by another cleric or by a lay person seems to leave room for an appraisal which regards the practice as sufficiently reasonable. The need for an accompanying cleric or layman arose both for the sake of reverence and for the protection of the administering priest. The cleric or lay person accompanied the minister to give notice, as it were, to the people that the priest was not to be disturbed, since he was in possession of the Holy Eucharist, and that the people themselves should manifest reverence to the sacrament. In the capacity of a guide or protector the accompanying person led the priest through the proper streets, and assisted him when perchance the roads were bad. Furthermore he could be of service in warding off curious or evil intentioned non-Catholics.

But now, in our present day circumstances, the priest in many instances uses the automobile to reach the stricken person, if the person is at all distant from the Church. The priest's use of the car eliminates to a great extent the danger of any irreverence which could come from passersby and others, and at the same time the use of the automobile provides for the Blessed Sacrament enough security from evil-intentiond non-Catholics. If the priest himself does not drive and the sick-call is to be made at some distance, then usually he will have someone drive him to the stricken person, and thus he will fulfill the prescript of the *Ritual* which bids him to be accompanied. If the sick-call is near to the church, then the priest walks to the stricken person, and usually the people in the immediate vicinity of the church realize and recognize rather readily that he is carrying the Blessed Sacrament.

Then, too, it seems that a serious inconvenience may be brought on the person who is asked to accompany the priest. In our present

---

reprobentur, tanquam iuris corruptelae corrigantur, licet sint immemorabiles, neve sinantur in posterum reviviscere; aliae, quae quidem centenariae sint et immemorabiles, tolerari poterunt, si Ordinarii pro locorum ac personarum adiunctis existiment eas prudenter submoveri non posse; ceterae suppressae habeantur, nisi expresse Codex aliud caveat.

circumstances it would be difficult to call anyone on short notice to accompany the priest. People are burdened with a daily routine of work, of study, or of other chores to such an extent that to call upon a person for his service of accompanying the priest even for a short time would entail in most cases a serious inconvenience for the person to whom such a request is served. This seems to reflect the normal experience in most instances; however, if a person is available, and suffers no inconvenience through his attendance, then by all means he should accompany the priest.

In certain instances the priest should be accompanied by another person. Such instances obtain if there would be a sick-call to a house of ill-repute, or a night sick-call. In the latter case one of the persons calling the priest to such an emergency call should take the priest to the stricken person; if that is not possible, then some other means should be used for obtaining the services of an accompanying person, or, if circumstances permit, the sick-call should be postponed until the morning hours. In cases of necessity and emergency *epikeia* can be lawfully used.

In general, therefore, under the present circumstances the practice seems to reflect valid excusing causes in warrant of its continuance. It may also be added that the same practice prevails in the city of Rome, and until the present time no decree of the Holy See has inveighed against the practice as it is current there.[121]

However, the practice of not wearing the proper vestments in the sick-room while administering Holy Viaticum does not seem to be attended with any just or reasonable cause which could duly warrant the continuance of that practice. This statement seems particularly convincing in the light of the decrees of the II Plenary Council of Baltimore and of the replies of the Sacred Congregation of Rites, both of which condemned this practice. Certainly no considerable inconvenience, either on the part of the priest or on the side of the sick person and his attendants, is sustained in the consequence of the priest's wearing the proper vestments. In the sick-call to a Catholic family the priest's appearance in proper vestments certainly would add to the devotion and reverence which are due the Blessed Sacrament on the part of the faithful. Furthermore

[121] Vermeersch-Creusen, *Epitome Iuris Canonici*, II, n. 114, 2.

the priest is bound by obedience to the *Ritual,* to the Code, and to the decree of the Council of Baltimore, to manifest external reverence to the sacrament, and this can be specifically done by the wearing of the proper vestments.

Yet, in certain instances in which the priest sincerely believed that irreverence or perhaps even an uneasy apprehension or alarm would be occasioned by the priest's appearance in a cassock, etc., he could by the use of *epikeia* dispense with the wearing of the regularly called for vestments. Such cases usually exist in connection with sick-calls to non-Catholic institutions, such as an asylum, a hospital, or a jail. There the use of the vestments could readily occasion irreverence and disrespect not only to the Blessed Sacrament Itself, but to religion in general.

Since in its various rites the Church strives to have unity in its liturgical laws, it seems that a weightier cause needs to be postulated if a practice is to become established as a legal custom in opposition to the liturgical law than when the custom stands contrary to other disciplinary laws in the Church. In addition, the liturgy of the Church reflects an intimate contact with the very sense and tenor of a well-disciplined orderliness within the Church. Customs contrary to liturgical law could readily disrupt the sense of discipline and undermine the purport of order within the Church. But canonists are agreed that any attending factor of such a disrupting or undermining character generally causes a practice to be unreasonable, and thus stands in the way of its becoming legitimately established. They feel that any reasonableness in such a factor would have to derive from an exceptionally imperative consideration. The writer believes that no such consideration is present to warrant a priest's disregard at random of the prescript which insists on the wearing of the proper vestments in the sick-room.

The canonists and the moralists, although they discuss at great length such practices as the priest's wearing of a hat while on a sick-call, or his riding in a public vehicle, and also other incidentals which may detract from the reverence due to the sacrament, remain strangely silent about the practice of not wearing the proper vestments in the sick-room. If there were any claim to make in favor of the licitness of such a practice, then one could certainly expect that the writers would have reflected their opinion regarding this particular practice, just as they did with reference to the other practices. One must accordingly conclude that their silence derived from but one or the other of two possible contingencies: either they abstracted from the very notion of the existence of such a practice at all, or, if they recognized the fact of its existence, they felt that no doubt could be raised regarding its unlawfulness. Inasmuch as it is not likely that they were not conscious of the existence of the practice in various places, it appears that they remained silent about the practice for the simple reason that no argument could be furnished in warrant of its at least probably lawful character, whether in view of the liturgical law itself, or in the light of any established contrary legal custom.

CHAPTER V

The Minister of Extreme Unction

Article 1. The Valid Minister

Canon 938, § 1: Hoc sacramentum valide administrat omnis et solus sacerdos.

For the valid administration of the sacrament of extreme unction the minister must be a priest. As before the promulgation of the Code so also now the administration by others who are not priests, regardless of whether they are major or minor clerics, or lay persons, is expressly prohibited by the present legislation of the Code. There is no doubt whatever that an administration by anyone other than a priest is invalid.

Since the canon mentions that every priest can validly administer the sacrament, it follows that excommunicated, suspended, and interdicted priests can likewise do so. However, these censured priests may not administer the sacrament at random. The urgency of the need for the reception of the sacrament and the severity of the penalty to which the priest is subject are factors which must be taken into consideration.[1]

In the Latin Church extreme unction is conferred at the hands of one priest to the exclusion of associate ministers. The *Roman Ritual* leaves place for but a single minister in the administration of this sacrament.[2] However, one can envision a case of necessity in which more than one priest could be employed for the performance of the actual sacramental rite. If, for example, a patient were so near to death that the anointings could not be completed in time by one priest, then, if several priests were present, they could by simultaneous actions complete the sacramental rite.[3] In

---

[1] Cf. *supra*, pp. 82-83.

[2] Tit. V, capp. 1 & 2.

[3] Noldin-Schmitt, *Summa Theologiae Moralis*, III, n. 439, b; Kilker, *Extreme Unction*, p. 91.

such a case, however, one of the priests would more readily use the single unction with the general form.[4]

Another case of necessity could occur if the priest while ministering the last sacrament suddenly became ill or died. In such an instance a second priest should complete the rite, provided that there is a moral unity between the breaking off and the continuance of the unctions. It is suggested that, if a space of fifteen minutes or more has elapsed, it would be more safe to repeat whatever unctions had been previously administered.[5]

It is generally held that a priest cannot administer extreme unction to himself, although he can administer Holy Viaticum to himself. Ecclesiastical history adduces perhaps no examples at all of a priest administering the sacrament to himself. This clearly indicates that there is in the Church a firm persuasion, as derived from an unbroken tradition, that a self administration of the sacrament of extreme unction is as equally impossible as self-absolution in the sacrament of penance. Furthermore, inasmuch as the sacrament of extreme unction is the complement of the sacrament of penance, and since a priest cannot administer the latter to himself, there is an inherent presumption against any priest's capability of anointing himself. A specific decree of the Congregation for the Propagation of the Faith explicitly ruled out the possibility of the self-administration of the sacrament of extreme unction.[6]

ARTICLE 2. THE LICIT MINISTER

Canon 938, § 2: Salvo praescripto can. 397, n. 3, 514, §§ 1-3, minister ordinarius est parochus loci, in quo degit

[4] Cf. canon 947, § 1: Unctiones verbis, ordine et modo in libris ritualibus praescripto, accurate peragantur; in casu autem necessitatis sufficit unica unctio in uno sensu seu rectius in fronte cum praescripta forma breviori, salva obligatione singulas unctiones supplendi, cessante periculo.

[5] Kilker, *op. cit.*, p. 92; Noldin-Schmitt, *loc. cit.*, Augustine, *A Commentary on Canon Law*, IV, 407-408; Gury-Ferreres, *Casus Conscientiae* (2 vols., *Barcinone*, 1921), II, 786.

[6] 23 martii 1844— ". . . inspectis ipsis divini eloquii verbis, vel facile patet, sacramentum Extremae Unctionis etiam in casu necessitatis, absente nimirum alio presbytero, non posse missionarium aegrotantem sibimetipsi ministrare." —*F. Lucii Ferraris Promptae Bibliothecae Supplementum* (ed. a Ianuario Bucceroni, Romae, 1899) s.v. *Extrema Unctio*, n. 4, p. 362.

> infirmus; in casu autem necessitatis, vel de licentia saltem rationabiliter praesumpta eiusdem parochi vel Ordinarii loci, alius quilibet sacerdos hoc sacramentum ministrare potest.

Just as the administration of Holy Viaticum is a parochial function, so also is the pastor the ordinary minister of extreme unction. The administration of this last sacrament belongs to him in virtue of his being a pastor. Since he possesses this power as an ordinary adjunct of his office, he may commit its use to others either for all cases alike or for individual cases only. The ordinary minister of extreme unction is the local pastor, and not simply the proper pastor of the stricken man. The local pastor's power extends over all the sick within the limits of his parish, whether they be his own subjects,[7] or sojourning visitors (*peregrini*), or persons who everywhere lack a domicile or even a quasi-domicile (*vagi*).[8]

Several exceptions are made by the Code. In the first place the administration of extreme unction to the bishop of the diocese is reserved by canon 397, n. 3, to the dignitaries and the canons of the cathedral chapter according to their order of precedence. In this country the diocesan consultors take the place of the dignitaries and canons of the cathedral chapter. Furthermore, in all clerical religious communities the superior has the right and duty to administer extreme unction, either in person or through another, to the professed, the novices, and to others who live day and night in the religious house, either as servants, or as students, or as guests, or also as patients and convalescents.

In the house of nuns, the ordinary confessor, or the one who takes his place, has the same right. In other laical organizations of religious this right and duty belongs to the pastor, or to the chaplain to whom the ordinary has given full parochial powers, in accordance with canon 464. Although they are not explicitly excepted in canon 938, § 2, yet all persons who reside in a seminary must also be regarded as exempt from parochial jurisdiction, and should receive the last sacraments from the rector of the seminary.[9]

---

[7] Cf. canon 94.

[8] Cf. canon 91.

[9] Cf. canon 1368.

In a case of necessity any priest may minister extreme unction with at least the presumed permission of the local ordinary or of the local pastor. The commentary which relates to the minister of Holy Viaticum applies also to the minister of extreme unction.[10]

---

[10] Cf. *supra*, pp. 71-81; 84-86.

CHAPTER VI

The Minister's Obligation to Administer the Last Sacraments

Laymen have the right to receive from the clergy, in so far as ecclesiastical regulations permit, spiritual benefits and especially the means necessary to salvation.[1] All who belong to the Church have a title to the means of sanctification it possesses; and on the legitimately constituted dispensers of these means the obligation of imparting them is imposed. The obligation to minister the sacraments in general can arise from justice or charity, depending on who the minister in a particular case may be. The ordinary minister is bound to administer the sacraments from justice, and the extraordinary minister from charity.

In regard to the administration of the last sacraments the local pastor is the ordinary minister, and he is bound *ex iustitia* to administer them.[2] Although the Code grants the person in danger of death the privilege to confess to any priest and to receive absolution from any sin or censure,[3] yet in virtue of canon 468, § 1, the pastor is at the same time bound in justice to hear the confession of the person in danger of death, if the circumstances are such that another priest is unavailable, or if the person does not wish to avail himself of the privilege granted by the Code. The pastor holds charge of his people, in virtue of which he receives the sustenance, or at least the honor, of a pastor with the obligation of performing those duties which ordinarily are proper to the office of the pastor. Among the pastor's duties the administration of the sacraments, particularly the last sacraments, is preeminent.[4]

---

[1] Canon 682.

[2] Cf. canon 468, § 1:—Sedula cura et effusa caritate debet parochus aegrotos in sua paroecia, maxime vero morti proximos, adiuvare, eos sollicite Sacramentis reficiendo eorumque animas Deo commendando. Cf. canons 850; 938, § 2.

[3] Cf. canon 882.

[4] Cf. canon 467.

It need hardly be mentioned that the obligation of the dignitaries and canons of the cathedral chapter,[5] or of the diocesan consultors, as well as of the various priests mentioned in canon 514, and of the seminary rector, arises likewise from justice, for they are all really ordinary ministers of the sacrament in regard to certain particular subjects.

All priests who are charged with the care of souls are bound under pain of mortal sin to assist all who are committed to their charge and to administer to them the last sacraments, unless a just cause excuses.[6] It such a priest culpably does not administer the last sacraments, he refuses to perform his duty to which he is bound by justice, and the consequence points to the presence of a mortal sin. The gravity of the sin is measured by the extent of the spiritual loss that is likely to arise from the failure to administer the last sacraments, and the loss thus sustainable can defy all calculation.

The question arises: Under what incommodity is the pastor bound to administer the last sacraments? Theologians commonly hold that pastors are bound even at the risk of their own lives to administer the sacraments which are absolutely necessary for eternal salvation. Hence, since the only absolutely necessary sacrament for non-Catholics not baptized validly is baptism, and for Catholics in mortal sin penance, it can hardly be said that the pastor is obliged at the same serious risk to confer Holy Viaticum and extreme unction.[7] The pastor is not held by the same grave obligation to minister Holy Viaticum or extreme unction, since in and of themselves these two sacraments are not absolutely necessary for salva-

---

[5] Cf. canon 397, n. 3.

[6] Fanfani, *De Iure Parochorum*, n. 229; Coronata, *De Sacramentis*, I, 43-45; Noldin-Schmitt, *Summa Theologiae Moralis*, III, 29.

[7] Coronata, *De Sacramentis*, I, 44-46; Cappello, *De Sacramentis*, I, n. 54 sqq.; Vermeersch, *Theologia Moralis*, III, n. 181; Noldin-Schmitt, *Summa Theologiae Moralis*, III, 30-31; Fanfani, *De Iure Parochorum*, n. 229; Kilker, *Extreme Unction*, p. 107; Prümmer, *Manuale Theologiae Moralis*, III, n. 73. Suarez (1548-1617) insisted, however, that the obligation of administering Viaticum at the peril of the pastor's own life is a grave one.—*Opera Omnia*, Disp. XLIV, *De Praeceptis et Ritu Sacramenti Extremae Unctionis*, sect. III, nn. 17-20—XXII, 873-877.

tion. As the case will be discussed later, the sacrament of extreme unction can in consequence of certain attendant circumstances become an absolute necessity for salvation. Although it is dear to the heart of the Good Shepherd for a pastor to dare all in order that his flock may obtain the salutary graces of all the sacraments, nevertheless the pastor is bound to risk his life for his subjects only when their spiritual lives are seriously endangered. This is surely not the case when the stricken person has already confessed and been absolved.

It is to be noted, however, that when the pastor can neutralize the danger to his own life or at least reduce it to a negligible consideration through the use of disinfectants and the like, he is bound to employ these and to confer the sacraments. The advantages derivable from the reception of all of the last sacraments are so preponderant that special inconveniences must be suffered for the purpose of their administration in these unusual circumstances. The employment of preventive measures is not too much to expect of one who has an obligation to care for the spiritual needs of his parish. He must cope with the contingencies of extraordinary situations in a reasonable fashion. When only reasonably much is demanded for overcoming the dangers on these occasions, he is required to put himself in inconveniences which are proportionate to the benefits which the souls under his charge will receive as a result of his trouble. The immense advantages that accrue to the sick person through the potent graces of Holy Viaticum and extreme unction certainly demand that no slight pains be taken by those who have the charge of souls in order to remove the causes which otherwise might excuse them from bestowing these two sacraments.

There is also the common opinion that if extreme unction incidentally becomes the only hope of salvation, e.g., when the stricken person has not been to confession for a long time and can be absolved only conditionally in view of his state of unconsciousness, then there is a grave obligation on the part of the pastor to administer extreme unction even at the peril of his own life.[8]

[8] Fanfani, *De Iure Parochorum,* n. 229; Noldin-Schmitt, *Summa Theologiae Moralis,* III, 30; Genicot-Salsmans, *Institutiones Theologiae Moralis,* II, 119 & 421; Coronata, *De Sacramentis,* I, 44 & 45; 595.

The reason is, of course, that the sacrament of extreme unction gives sanctifying grace to those who the while they have attrition for their sins cannot make a confession. Extreme unction is left as the only means of assisting the dying man. The practice which is followed in cases wherein the person is unconscious and cannot confess is that of granting a conditional absolution and of thereupon administering absolutely the sacrament of extreme unction.[9]

Before a priest is strictly bound to endanger his life in behalf of a soul under his care, it is necessary that there be verified all the conditions which taken together give rise to the heroic duty. In the first place, it is necessary that the subject be truly in grave peril of his eternal salvation. Secondly, the means which the priest has at his command must be certainly sufficient to relieve the patient from his necessity. Moreover, the hope of rescuing the stricken person must be morally assured, and, finally, no graver evils must result from the administration undertaken by the priest. If any of these conditions is lacking, then the severity of the obligation is relaxed.

Authors classify the peril to the loss of eternal salvation under three headings:

1. A person is said to be in extreme danger of losing his eternal salvation if it is practically certain that he will lose his eternal life without the help of another person. Infants dying without baptism, infidels and heretics who are in danger of death, persons near death who while unconscious are in the state of mortal sin, persons near death who, though they be conscious the while they are in the state of mortal sin, nevertheless do not know that an act of contrition is imperatively necessary, or do not know how to elicit this act of sorrow—all these persons are considered to be in extreme danger of losing their salvation. In such cases the pastor is bound *ex iustitia* to administer at the risk of his own life either baptism, penance (absolutely or conditionally), or extreme unction, according as the case may demand. And if the risk to his

[9] Coronata notes that as often as extreme unction can be administered a sacramental absolution can likewise be given conditionally; however, he states that the derived effects of extreme unction are better certified under these circumstances than the effects of the conditional absolution.—*De Sacramentis,* I, 44, footnote n. 7.

life is lessened in any considerable degree, the pastor would be bound to administer Holy Viaticum too.

2. A person is said to be in grave danger of losing his eternal salvation when he can be of spiritual help to himself only with great difficulty, thus making his chances for salvation improbable without the assistance of another person. A sinner, for example, who is near death and has neglected to live a good Catholic life throughout his entire life would in all probability be in such grave peril. Here the priest would be bound just as much as in the case of extreme danger to administer whichever sacraments the circumstances would permit. Authors maintain that, when a general status of grave necessity is present in any communities, then there, also exists a status of extreme necessity, for among all those who are near death there surely is present also a number of persons who are in extreme danger of losing their eternal lives.[10]

3. Finally, the danger of the loss of salvation is termed a common danger when the faithful in considerable numbers are confronted with it at the time of death. Such a danger could without great difficulty be counteracted by the person himself by means of an act of contrition, since the person in this classification is aware of the need of contrition, and can easily enough elicit it. The priest is not bound to risk his life to minister the sacraments to such persons, since they are not in an extreme or even any grave danger of losing their salvation. However, once the peril to the priest's own life is no longer present or has been notably mitigated, then he is bound by a grave obligation of justice to administer the last sacraments.

Accordingly, if the priest is morally certain that the sick man is in the state of grace, either because he has not sinned since his last confession or because he has successfully elicited an act of perfect contrition, he is excused from risking his life in administering the last sacraments. If he knows nothing or is in doubt about the state of conscience of the sick man, then Suarez held that a priest is obligated to hazard even the certain danger of death in order to administer the last sacraments.[11] Later authors are not

---

[10] Noldin-Schmitt, *Summa Theologiae Moralis,* III, 31; Coronata, *De Sacramentis,* I, 45.

[11] *Opera Omnia,* Disp. XLIV, *De Praeceptis et Ritu Sacramenti Extremae Unctionis,* sect. III, n. 15—XXII, 873.

so exacting as Suarez. They demand not moral certainty, but simple probability that the sick person be in the state of grace, if the minister is to feel rightfully excused from the obligation of risking his life in the administering of the sacraments.[12] There is certainly enough authority for a pastor to follow the milder opinion. He can refuse to enter a *certain* danger of death under every circumstance in which the absolute need of his assistance to the sick man is not evident. The deduction of Vermeersch (1858-1936), who predicated the uncertainty of the sick man's dispositions in every case wherein the sick man is unconscious, appears too broad a statement. A fair indication of the internal dispositions can at least sometimes be obtained even though the dying person be unconscious.

Moreover, the successful outcome of the administration by the pastor must be morally certain. Hence, if the priest sees that he will probably be hindered from administering the sacraments, he is not bound to undergo a certain imperiling of his life. Similarly, if he feels that he will not reach the sick person in time, and that his attempt to do so will probably prove fatal to himself (as in times of persecution), then he is released from the strict obligation of attendance.[13]

Finally, if it is foreseen that greater evils will result from the administering than from the non-administering of the last sacraments, then the priest is not bound to submit himself to such an inevitable jeopardy of life. Private good must cede to the common good. Hence, if the pastor knows that by his death the salvation of the community will no longer be sufficiently provided for because of the lack of priests, he is excused from hazarding his life at such a cost.[14]

[12] Cappello, *De Sacramentis,* I, n. 54:—"Non teneretur parochus aliusve certo periculo vitae se exponere, si probabiliter putaret, ex. gr., moribundum . . . non reperiri in statu culpae mortalis vel sibimet consulere posse per contritionem perfectam." Cf. Fanfani, *De Iure Parochorum,* n. 229; Vermeersch, *Theologia Moralis,* III, nn. 181, 610.

[13] Cf. Fanfani, *De Iure Parochorum,* n. 229; Cappello, *De Sacramentis,* I, n. 54.

[14] Suarez, *Opera Omnia,* Disp. XLIV, *De Praeceptis et Ritu Sacramenti Extremae Unctionis,* sect. III, n. 15—XXII, 873; Vermeersch, *Theologia Moralis,* III, n. 181.

This set of circumstances arises often in missionary lands, where very few priests are working among great numbers of the faithful.

Just as the certain and complete fulfillment of every condition is necessary before a strict obligation rests on the pastor when the danger is serious and certain, so a solidly probable realization of these identical conditions must be present if there is to arise any rigid responsibility to minister the last sacraments when the administration entails probable danger of death to the priest.[15] In order, then, that the pastor must risk a probable danger of death, it is necessary that the subject be probably in grave peril of losing his eternal salvation and that the success of the pastor's venture can be hoped for with a strong degree of probability.[16]

In a summary manner it may be stated that, if it is morally certain that the patient will not attain salvation except through the ministration of the priest, and if there is moral certainty of the successful outcome of the priest's attempt to confer the sacraments, then a priest who has charge of souls is bound in justice to brave the certain danger of death, and even death itself, to confer the sacraments upon the stricken person. If the person is conscious, then at least the sacrament of penance must be administered, and if at all possible also Holy Viaticum and extreme unction. If, however, the person is unconscious, then conditional absolution and extreme unction should be administered if the circumstances permit it. However, if the common good will subsequently suffer through the loss of the priest, the advantage that will accrue to the particular individual must be regarded in relation to the greater good that will be gained by the community. Hence, in such a case a priest is released from this severe obligation. Indeed, he may often be bound not to attend a sick person, for example, when he is sure that his risking of life will seriously imperil the eternal salvation of many others in the community.

Next is considered the priest's obligation of administering extreme unction as well as conditional absolution in the cases con-

---

[15] Cappello, *De Sacramentis,* I, n. 54:—"Eadem regula . . . valet quoque congrua congruis referendo, ubi agitur de gravi necessitate, ob quam sacramenta ministranda sunt cum periculo gravi et probabili sanitatis aut vitae."

[16] Vermeersch, *Theologia Moralis,* III, n. 181:—"Si solummodo probabilis sit successus vel necessitas, obligatio pro pastore manet quidem cum probabili vitae periculo."

templated in canon 941.[17] The pastor is bound to anoint conditionally a child who has only doubtfully attained the use of reason. In practice a previous conditional absolution is granted likewise. The obligation is a grave one, so that only a very serious inconvenience excuses from it.[18]

It stands to reason, however, that a priest is not bound to enter the same degree of peril in order to give the sacrament to a child who only probably needs it as he would be obliged to do for an adult who certainly needs it for his salvation. Nevertheless, the child has more than a probable right to a conditional administration by the priest. Only by the priest's administration is the child sure of its salvation, and its title to the means which will ensure its salvation is not only probable, but certain. Accordingly, since the child's claim upon the priest is certain, the priest is obligated under serious inconvenience to do all for the salvation of this soul in his charge.

In regard to the pastor's obligation in the case of those who are doubtfully in danger of death, it may be stated that, if while the danger is still doubtful there is any likelihood that the spiritual welfare of the patient will not be sufficiently secured except by means of a conditional administration of extreme unction as well as by either an absolute or a conditional administration of the sacrament of penance according as the attendant circumstances may dictate and also by the administration of Holy Viaticum if the circumstances permit it, then the pastor is bound *sub gravi* to give extreme unction conditionally, and the other sacraments as soon as possible. If, however, the delay which is required for determining the exact status of the sick person will not be of any great detriment to the sick person, then it cannot be said that any grave obligation rests on the minister until a certain danger of death does appear.[19]

The third case mentioned in canon 941 is that in which there is doubt whether or not the person is already dead. For such per-

[17] "Quando dubitatur num infirmus usum rationis attigerit, num in periculo mortis reipsa versetur vel num mortuus sit, hoc sacramentum ministretur sub conditione."

[18] Lehmkuhl, *Theologia Moralis,* II, 723; Gury-Ferreres, *Casus Conscientiae,* II, n. 799; Kilker, *Extreme Unction,* p. 112.

[19] Kilker, *Extreme Unction,* p. 115.

sons, unable as they are to confess and to receive Holy Viaticum, a conditional absolution and the conferring of the sacrament of extreme unction will remain the only means of spiritual assistance which through the sacraments the minister can grant. Thus extreme unction incidentally becomes an absolutely necessary sacrament of salvation, if these persons are in the state of mortal sin.

The solution would be easy if the patient were certainly known to be but apparently dead. Life's dissolution would not yet have truly occurred, and the person would still be a *viator,* thus having a claim upon the pastor's services as much as the other persons who are under his care. But there is no certainty in this case, and consequently the solution of the case must depend on principles of probability. While the man is probably alive, he has a right to the sacraments, provided all the other conditions necessary are present. Consequently the pastor is bound to administer to the souls in his care, for they have a claim to his attention especially in these urgent cases. Their title to a conditional administration of extreme unction is reasserted in canon 941 with the words: *ministretur sub conditione.*

Accordingly the ordinary minister of extreme unction is bound in justice to bestow this conditional administration, and similarly a duty in charity is imposed upon the extraordinary ministers. Where there is a solid probability that the man is not yet dead, the obligation to give extreme unction and absolution conditionally, even at the cost of grave inconvenience, is seriously binding on the ordinary minister. It is the consensus of theologians that a man is very probably alive for a half-hour after his apparent death in a lingering illness, and from an hour to two hours after his apparent death which has resulted from sudden illness, accident, etc.[20] Hence a priest who has the care of souls is under a grave obligation to administer to the apparently dead person for a half hour after apparent death has resulted from a lingering disease or illness, and for about two hours after apparent death has resulted from a sudden illness or accident. Extreme unction should be administered

---

[20] Cappello, *De Sacramentis,* III, 168-171; Noldin-Schmitt, *Summa Theologiae Moralis,* III, 301; Gury-Ferreres, *Casus Conscientiae,* II, 1213; Kern, *Tractatus de Extrema Unctione,* p. 322; Vermeersch, *Theologia Moralis,* III, n. 610; Kilker, *Extreme Unction,* p. 114; Genicot-Salsmans, *Institutiones Theologiae Moralis,* II, 422.

to such a person conditionally under the form *Si vivis*. In practically all cases only a single unction should be made; if the person survives the extant imminent danger of death, then the other unctions are to be supplied.

The administration of the last sacraments can be fulfilled by any priest who receives the permission of the pastor. Consequently, though the pastor is bound to formal residence in his parish in times of a plague, yet he is not bound to the personal administration in all the cases that come under his charge. However, purposely to circumvent the peril of a contagious disease, or any other danger to his life and to refrain completely from the administration of the last sacraments would be a serious and deliberate neglect of one of his primary duties as pastor.

Noldin (1838-1922) and others held the opinion that, if the dying man asks for the pastor expressly, then the pastor is obligated to attend him personally unless he be impeded by a more serious duty.[21] However, others believed that since the strict letter of the law allows a fulfillment of the obligation through some other minister, the pastor is not bound in justice to a personal administration of the sacraments.[22] It is, of course, most desirable that the pastor should go himself if he is personally summoned.

In cases of extreme spiritual need any priest is bound *sub gravi* out of charity to administer the necessary sacraments even at the risk of losing his own life. Theologians maintain that beyond this case of extreme necessity he is not bound to risk his life to assist the stricken person.[23] Zeal will dictate that the priest ordinarily be most earnest and helpful to the persons who are in need of the sacraments, no matter how great or how small the need for the administration of the necessary sacraments may be in each case. Each case supposes, of course, that there is not at hand any priest who is bound out of justice to do this work. If he is present and willing to administer the sacrament, then there is no obligation on the priest who has not the care of souls.

---

[21] *Summa Theologiae Moralis*, III, 30; Vermeersch, *Theologia Moralis*, III, n. 181; Cappello, *De Sacramentis*, I, n. 54.

[22] Genicot-Salsmans, *Institutio Theologiae Moralis*, II, 119; Coronata, *De Sacramentis*, I, 45; Kilker, *Extreme Unction*, p. 117.

[23] Coronata, *De Sacramentis*, I, 46; Vermeersch, *Theologia Moralis*, III, n. 181; Cappello, *De Sacramentis*, I, n. 54.

CHAPTER VII

The Minister of the Last Sacraments and Incidental Questions

Article 1. The Subject of the Last Sacraments

Before anyone may receive the sacraments of penance, Holy Communion, and extreme unction, he must not only have received a valid baptism, but he must also have attained the use of reason.[1] The age of discretion for the reception of Holy Communion is the same as the age of discretion which is postulated for the reception of sacramental absolution.[2]

In order that a person may avail himself according to the ruling of canon 882, of the privilege of having any sin or censure absolved by any priest, he must be in danger of death.[3] The same is true of the reception of Holy Viaticum. All the faithful who are in danger of death are urged both by divine and ecclesiastical law to receive Holy Communion under the form of Viaticum.[4]

---

[1] Cf. canon 906: Omnis utriusque sexus fidelis, postquam ad annos discretionis, idest ad usum rationis, pervenerit, tenetur omnia peccata sua saltem semel in anno fideliter confiteri. Canon 859, § 1: Omnis utriusque sexus fidelis, postquam ad annos discretionis, idest ad rationis usum, pervenerit, debet semel in anno saltem in Paschate, Eucharistiae sacramentum recipere. . . . Canon 940, § 1: Extrema unctio praeberi non potest nisi fideli, qui post adeptum usum rationis ob infirmitatem vel senium in periculo mortis versetur.

[2] S. C. de Sacramentis, decr. 8 aug. 1910: "Quos reprehendimus abusus ex eo sunt repetendi, quod nec scite nec recte definiverint quaenam sit aetas discretionis qui aliam Poenitentiae, aliam Eucharistiae assignarunt. Unam tamen eandemque aetatem ad utrumque Sacramentum requirit Lateranense Concilium, quum coniunctum Confessionis et Communionis onus imponit."—*AAS,* II (1910), 580; *Fontes,* n. 2103; Crotty, *The Recipient of First Holy Communion,* The Catholic University of America Canon Law Studies, n. 247 (Washington, D. C.: The Catholic University of America Press, 1947), pp. 35-54.

[3] Cf. *supra,* pp. 49-51.

[4] Cf. St. John, VI :54; canon 864, § 1: "In periculo mortis, quavis ex causa procedat, fideles sacrae communionis recipiendae praecepto tenentur."

The danger of death which suffices for the application of the ruling contained in canon 882 and for the administration of Holy Viaticum may arise from a cause which is intrinsic or extrinsic to the recipient. This, however, is not the same in the case of extreme unction. The subject of extreme unction must be in danger of death from some infirmity or from old age—old age may be considered an infirmity—which danger actually affects the person at the time the sacrament is being administered.[5] Thus a condemned prisoner who while waiting for execution enjoys good health could receive Viaticum and use the privilege granted in canon 882, but he could not receive extreme unction. The same is true of soldiers before entering battle.[6]

For the reception of sacramental absolution of Holy Viaticum, and of extreme unction an implicit habitual intention is required on the part of the subject. A habitual intention is one which, though once elicited and never revoked, nevertheless does not actually influence the act when it is placed. An implicit intention regarding the reception of the last sacraments is an elicited act of the will which simply tends to the exercise of a conduct in accord with the teachings and the commandments of Christ and the Church.[7] Since a habitual intention suffices, it follows *a fortiori* that an actual or virtual intention is more than sufficient.

But for the sacrament of penance a habitual intention does not prove sufficient. According to the more common opinion, the matter of this sacrament consists of the acts of the penitent. But these acts cannot exist apart from a virtual intention of receiving the sacrament.[8]

In regard to the subject's right to be absolved when he is in danger of death, notice must be taken of the fact that the dying penitent is excused from making a materially integral confession

---

[5] Cf. canon 940, § 1; O'Kane-Fallon, *Notes on the Rubrics of the Roman Ritual* (4. ed., Dublin: Duffy, 1938), p. 453.

[6] Cf. S. C. de Prop. Fide (C. P. pro Sin.—Tunkin. Occident.), 21 iul. 1841, ad 1 et 2—*Fontes*, n. 4789; S. C. de Prop. Fide (C. P. pro Sin.), 20 febr. 1801—*Fontes*, n. 4662.

[7] Noldin-Schmitt, *Summa Theologiae Moralis*, I, 53; Coronata, *De Sacramentis*, I, 34-37; Aertnys-Damen, *Theologia Moralis*, II, 32.

[8] Coronata, *De Sacramentis*, I, 65.

if he is physically or morally unable to do so. Hence if a person became unconscious after confessing one or several of his sins, such a person should nevertheless be absolved absolutely. So also, if the stricken person cannot make a complete long confession without grave harm to his health or without other great difficulty, he should be given absolution after he has confessed whatever sins he could confess short of any grave harm or great difficulty. Or if the stricken person cannot make a complete examination of conscience because of some mental illness or head injury, then the priest should grant absolution despite the fact that the penitent's confession does not reflect a thorough examination of conscience. If the seriously ill penitent confesses in a general manner by acknowledging the fact that he sinned and is sorry (either in a few words or through signs), then too absolution is to be given. The absolution should be absolute, unless for some other reason a conditional absolution is to be employed. In all these cases it must be remembered, however, that whatever sins were left unmentioned must later be confessed at a time when a fit opportunity presents itself.[9]

The proper dispositions necessary for a valid absolution are always to be presumed in those dying persons who have lost consciousness, unless the priest is morally certain that such is not the case. Thus the following would be absolved conditionally:

1) those who lived good Christian lives, although before lapsing from consciousness they did not give any sign of repentance;

2) also those persons who did not live good Christian lives, although they remained at least nominally Catholics. It is safe to presume that such people desired to die as Christians. This presumption is based on their not denouncing their faith or leaving it. In addition to the desire of dying as Christians they also may have elicited an act of contrition before they lapsed from consciousness. Such penitents who have lapsed from consciousness could at times have a lucid interval at which time they could make an act of contrition. Such an act may be noticed by onlookers or by the minister himself through the penitent's weak aspirations, movements of the eyes, lips, or by some other perceptible signs. Persons

---

[9] Cf. Noldin-Schmitt, *Summa Theologiae Moralis,* III, 299-300.

in whose residences are found religious articles as holy cards, medals, pictures, scapulars, rosaries, etc., provide evidence that they were Catholics at least nominally even though they did not live good Catholic lives;

3) those Catholics who lost consciousness in the very act of sin, e.g., in a duel or in an attempt to inflict death upon themselves or others.

Among the authors there is not a unanimous agreement that favors the granting of conditional absolution to this last class of penitents. Nevertheless some authors hold it as a probable opinion that these last mentioned penitents may be absolved as long as the attending minister can judge with some degree of probability that the penitent showed sometime during his life signs of contrition, which contrition could have been recalled at the moment of the penitent's lapsing into unconsciousness and may have caused him to detest the sin that he had committed.[10]

It could appear that the sacrament is being exposed to the danger of invalidity, since it must be admitted that the presence of proper dispositions on the part of the penitent is not satisfactorily evident. Yet, although the sacrament should not be exposed to the danger of invalidity, the consideration of the law of charity in these extreme cases prevails over the consideration of the risk of administering the sacrament invalidly. The effort to save a soul from eternal damnation furnishes an excusing cause for inviting the attendant risk of administering invalidly the particular sacrament then and there in question.

Conditional absolution in these cases is possible, because perhaps before his lapse into unconsciousness there may have been a short interval during which the person may have realized the sinful state of his soul and the danger of eternal damnation, and having elicited an act of contrition he may have desired to become reconciled with God through absolution.

Absolution, however, must be refused to those in whom no rea-

---

[10] Cf. Merkelbach, *Quaestiones Pastorales* (6 vols., Vol. III, *Quaestiones de Variis Poenitentium Categoriis*—Liege, 1928), III, 98-100; Davis, *Moral and Pastoral Theology,* III, 256-257; Noldin-Schmitt, *Summa Theologiae Moralis,* III, 299-300.

sonable traces of sorrow or repentance can be found.[11] In this classification would be such persons who even up to the moment of lapsing into unconsciousness expressly rejected the assistance of the Church and its sacraments.[12]

Before a priest can absolve even conditionally, an externally manifested sorrow must be present in the penitent. Not only are those persons to be absolved absolutely who by words or some signs have manifested to the priest himself that they desire to confess and are sorry for their sins, but also those who in the absence of a priest manifested to some bystanders their desire to confess and their sense of sorrow. However, those who in only some tenably probable way have manifested their desire for confession are to be absolved conditionally. The moralists presume that the proper dispositions are present in such cases. The reason for this presumption is based on the fact that the person manifested externally his desire for the sacrament of penance by some action or sign which, although it did not explicitly point to a desire for confession or to an eliciting of sorrow, nevertheless may be construed as such. An aspiration or some other pious utterance may signify sorrow and the accompanying desire for absolution. The presumption may surely also derive from the fact that the person lived a good life. Even if the person made little positive effort to lead a good life, the very fact that he remained in the Church to the end of his life can be accepted as an external manifestation of his desire to effect at his death a reconciliation with God by means of the sacramental absolution of his sins.

Authors admit the difficulty of the apparent lack of an externally manifested sorrow in those who have lost consciousness in the very act of sin. The manifestation of the desire for absolution as based on the person's remaining a member of the Church until the end of his life seems to be revoked by the sin he has committed; sorrow apparently seems to be absent in the subject. Authors suggest various solutions for such cases, e.g., by insisting on the distinction between the sorrow which as a disposition was revoked by the sin and the sorrow which subsequent to the sin was mani-

[11] *Rituale Romanum,* Tit. V, cap. 1, n. 10:—". . . qui impoenitentes in manifesto peccato mortali contumaciter perseverant. . . ."

[12] Noldin-Schmitt, *Summa Theologiae Moralis,* III, 300.

fested by the will for the sin just committed. This subsequent sorrow would serve as a disposition sufficing for a conditional absolution.[13]

As to the time during which absolution is to be granted to apparently dead persons, the same norms are to be followed as in the administration of extreme unction to persons who are in the same set of circumstances.[14]

As to the recipient of the Holy Eucharist it should be noted that Holy Communion can be given to only those who enjoy the use of reason and who at the same time possess the requisite dispositions of body and soul. The recipient must be in the state of grace; he must have at least an explicit habitual, true and sincere desire to receive the sacrament. Furthermore, the recipient is required to know the difference between an unconsecrated host and the Sacred Species. The recipient must be able intelligently to appreciate the sacrament, which appreciation in turn should lead to a due measure of desire, reverence, devotion, and affection. At the same time cleanliness on the part of the recipient, of his attendants, and of his surroundings should be in evidence.[15]

It may be stated as a general rule that the conditions necessary for the fruitful reception of Viaticum are less exacting than those which are required for the reception of simple Holy Communion. The requisite state of grace demanded in all communicants alike is of course a point regarding which no difference obtains under any given circumstances. The Eucharist can never be fruitfully received by one who is in the state of mortal sin, except by a person who is in good faith.

Outside the danger of death an explicit intention of receiving the Eucharist is demanded, but an implicit intention suffices when the danger of death is present. The recipients of Viaticum are not required to observe the law of the natural fast.[16]

Neither uncleanliness of person, nor squalor of dress, nor

---

[13] Cf. Noldin-Schmitt, *Summa Theologiae Moralis,* III, 300-301; Lehmkuhl, *Theologia Moralis,* II, n. 650.

[14] Cf. *supra,* pp. 156 158.

[15] Crotty, *The Recipient of First Holy Communion,* pp. 55-72.

[16] Cf. canon 858, § 1.

wretchedness of living conditions stands inherently in the way of the reception of Viaticum.[17]

But when such conditions obtain it is not at all times warranted to administer Holy Viaticum to the victims of these conditions, for the *Roman Ritual* rules that Holy Communion should not be given when there is danger of irreverence to the Sacred Species.[18] To avoid needless repetition the writer wishes it to be understood that when, in the following paragraphs, it is stated that a certain type of abnormal persons may be admitted to receive Holy Viaticum, such persons may receive the sacrament provided that they possess the necessary qualifications, and provided that there is not present any danger of irreverence.

Those who have been totally insane from birth may not receive Holy Viaticum. In law such persons enjoy the standing of children who have not yet attained the years of discretion.[19] Consequently such persons are prohibited from the reception of Holy Viaticum. It may happen, however, that a person from birth is not totally but only partially insane. His insanity may be centered on some particular object, and consequently he may enjoy the outlook of a normal individual on other things. Authors agree that such a person may be allowed to communicate, provided that the special object of his insanity is not the Eucharist.[20]

Insane persons who enjoy lucid intervals may receive Holy Viaticum during the intervals when their mental disorder has abated.[21]

Authors agree that the Eucharist could not be administered to an insane person while he is actually suffering from the loss of

---

[17] Cf. Alexander VII, const. *Sacrosancti,* 18 ian. 1658, § 2, n. 13—*Fontes,* n. 235.

[18] Tit. IV, cap. 1, *de sanctissimo Eucharistiae sacramento,* n. 10: "Amentibus praeterea, seu phreneticis communicare non licet; licebit tamen, si quando habeant lucida intervalla, et devotionem ostendant, dum in eo statu manent, si nullum indignitatis periculum adsit."

[19] Cf. canon 88, § 3.

[20] Cf. Gasparri, *De Sanctissima Eucharistia,* II, 356; Cappello, *De Sacramentis,* I, 364; Coronata, *De Sacramentis,* I, 285; Regatillo, *Ius Sacramentarium,* I, 178.

[21] *Rituale Romanum,* Tit. IV, cap. 1, *de sanctissimo Eucharistiae sacramento,* n. 10.

reason. The exception is found in cases wherein the danger of death is present. Gasparri seems to doubt whether even Viaticum could be administered to such an individual, but he expressly refrains from condemning those who maintain that it is lawful to give Viaticum to a person who is actually insane, but who before losing the use of reason was properly disposed for Its reception.[22] The consensus of theologians is that those who once enjoyed the use of reason and who are actually insane at the time of danger of death may receive Viaticum if, while they were sane, they formed and never revoked at least an implicit intention of receiving the Eucharist.[23] The Catechism of the Council of Trent lends additional weight to the teaching of the theologians and canonists.[24]

However, since in these cases there may be a grave danger of irreverence, and since Holy Viaticum is not absolutely necessary for eternal salvation, in practice such persons are not usually communicated even when they are in danger of death.

There is another class of people who cannot be regarded as really insane, but who nevertheless cannot be regarded as normal persons. They enjoy the use of reason, but in a feeble manner (*semi-fatui*). Refusal or permission to receive Viaticum depends on the absence or presence of the requisite dispositions, as enumerated in canon 854, § 2.[25] It seems quite equitable to resolve in favor of the individual any doubt regarding the sufficiency of his dispo-

---

[22] *De Sanctissima Eucharistia,* II, 356.

[23] Suarez, *De Eucharistia,* q. 80, art. 9, disp. 68, sect. 6—*Opera Omnia,* XXI, 520; De Lugo, *De Sacramento Eucharistiae,* Disp. XIII, sect. 3, n. 24—*Disputationes Scholasticae et Morales,* IV, 59; Cappello, *De Sacramentis,* I, 364-365; Regatillo, *Ius Sacramentarium,* I, 179; Coronata, *De Sacramentis,* I, 285; Tanquerey, *Synopsis Theologiae Dogmaticae,* III, 655.

[24] "Quamvis si antequam in insaniam inciderent, piam et religiosam animi voluntatem praestulerunt, licebit eis in fine viatae, ex concilii Carthaginensis decreto, eucharistiam administrare, modo vomitionis vel alterius indignitatis et incommodi periculum nullum timendum est."—*Catechismus ex Decreto Concilii Tridentini ad Parochos Pii V Pontificis Max., et deinde Clementis XIII, Iussu Editus* (Taurini-Romae: Marietti, 1930), Pars II, *De Eucharistiae Sacramento,* n. 64.

[25] Canon 854, § 2:—In periculo mortis, ut sanctissima Eucharistia pueris ministrari possit ac debeat, satis est ut sciant Corpus Christi a communi cibo discernere illudque reverenter adorare.

sitions, according to the axiom, *"sacramenta propter homines."*[26] Noldin-Schmitt advise that the minister should not be scrupulous in administering the Eucharist in such cases.[27]

In regard to a person who is deaf, blind, and dumb, Holy Viaticum may be administered to him if he possesses the requisite qualifications for admission to Holy Communion.[28] In such cases the priest should resolve all doubts in favor of the sufficiency of the person's dispositions, as in the case of the feebleminded people.

Often the nature of the malady from which a person suffers when he is in danger of death through sickness keeps him from the reception of Holy Viaticum. The *Ritual* forbids the administration of the Eucharist when indignity to the Sacred Species is feared because of a frenzied state of the patient, or because of a persistent cough, or because of some other malady.[29]

The *Roman Ritual* definitely states that Holy Viaticum should be administered to a person while he is conscious.[30] Hence the administration of the sacrament to the unconscious appears not to be contemplated by the *Ritual.* Since the danger of irreverence is present in an administration to the unconscious, and since irreverence to the Host must always be avoided even if this means that an attempt to communicate a dying person cannot be made, the communicating of an unconscious person is at the least unadvisable.

The state of frenzy mentioned in the *Ritual* is usually understood as a state of mental derangement accompanied with violent physical action. The danger of irreverence to the Host is very frequently present in cases of frenzy, as it is often impossible to

---

[26] Vermeersch, *Theologia Moralis,* III, 175.

[27] *Summa Theologiae Moralis,* III, 138.

[28] Cappello, *De Sacramentis,* I, 366.

[29] Tit. IV, cap. 4, *de communione infirmorum,* n. 4:—"Potest quidem Viaticum brevi morituris dari non ieiunis; id tamen diligenter curandum est, ne iis tribuatur, a quibus ob phrenesim, sive ob assiduam tussim, aliumve similem morbum, aliqua indecentia cum iniuria tanti Sacramenti timeri potest."

[30] Tit. IV, cap. 4, *de communione infirmorum,* n. 2:—"Sanctum Viaticum infirmis ne nimium differatur; et qui animarum curam gerunt, sedulo advigilent ut eo infirmi plene sui compotes reficiantur."

predict the reactions which may follow the administration of the Eucharist. Noldin and others suggest that after an unconsecrated particle has been administered, and it is still uncertain that no danger of irreverence is present, Viaticum should not be administered.[81]

The presence of a persistent cough may or may not constitute a danger of irreverence. If the cough is so severe that as a result the patient is unable to swallow, then obviously no attempt to administer Viaticum should be made. But if the sick person is capable of swallowing the Host, or a small fraction thereof, Viaticum may be given. No danger of irreverence need be feared from the fact that the patient constantly expectorates phlegm. Phlegm which comes to the mouth as a result of severe coughing has its origin in the trachea, or the passage which leads to the lungs, and not in the esophagus, or the passage which leads to the stomach.

Vomiting may likewise exist as a cause of irreverence. Vomiting may result from the taking of food, or it may occur independently of eating or drinking. The use of an unconsecrated particle to test the patient's ability to retain the Host long enough for digestion is a satisfactory practical procedure. If vomiting does not occur for a half-hour after the unconsecrated particle is swallowed, the priest can be reasonably certain that no danger of irreverence is to be feared, and he can proceed to administer the sacrament.[82]

The practice of allowing children who have reached the use of reason to die without receiving Viaticum has been condemned as an utterly detestable abuse, and local ordinaries have been instructed to proceed severely against those who do not abandon the practice.[83] Children who enjoy the qualifications specified in canon 854, § 2, have a strict right to receive Viaticum.[84] Considerably

[81] *Summa Theologiae Moralis*, III, 138; Crotty, *The Recipient of First Holy Communion*, p. 103.

[82] Regatillo, *Ius Sacramentarium*, I, 179; O'Kane-Fallon, *Notes on the Rubrics of the Roman Ritual*, p. 400.

[83] S. C. de Sacr., decr. 8 aug. 1910, n. VIII—*AAS*, II (1910), 583; *Fontes*, n. 2103.

[84] Canon 854, § 2:—In periculo mortis, ut sanctissima Eucharistiae pueris ministrari possit ac debeat, satis est ut sciant Corpus Christi a communi cibo discernere illudque reverenter adorare.

less intellectual preparation for the reception of Viaticum is demanded by the Code than for the reception of Holy Communion outside the danger of death. Children receiving first Holy Communion by way of Viaticum are not required to have a knowledge of the mysteries of faith absolutely necessary for salvation.[35]

Occasionally the minister of the sacrament may doubt whether a child enjoys the requisite qualifications for admission to Viaticum. The best solution for the problem is the one commonly advocated by canonists, namely, that in such circumstances there is no strict obligation to administer Viaticum, though the minister is free to do so. They state that the more laudable practice is to administer the sacrament to such a child, since under the circumstances there is question of a law which is favorable to the child—"*favores convenit ampliari.*"[35a]

When it is doubted whether a child who is in danger of death has a sufficient knowledge for the reception of Viaticum, the pastor by virtue of canon 1330, 2°, has the obligation of preparing the child for the reception of Viaticum, which will then be received as first Holy Communion.[36] The obligation of the pastor arises from justice; other priests or also deacons, if called for some legitimate reason to attend the child, would be bound in charity not only to dispose the child for the reception of Viaticum but also to administer It.[37]

As was previously mentioned in regard to the administration of extreme unction, the subject must be in danger of death from sickness or old age. Furthermore, in the same illness this sacrament cannot be repeated unless the sick person rallies after the reception of the last anointing and his illness again becomes critical.[38]

---

[35] Cf. canon 854, § 3.

[35a] Cf. Noldin-Schmitt, *Summa Theologiae Moralis,* III, 143; Cappello, *De Sacramentis,* I, 399; McNicholas, "The Age of Children for First Communion"—*AER,* XLIII (1910), 487; O'Kane-Fallon, *Notes on the Rubrics of the Roman Ritual,* p. 319; Crotty, *The Recipient of First Holy Communion,* pp. 106-107.

[36] Canon 1330, 2° :—Debet parochus: Peculiari omnino studio, praesertim, si nihil obsit, Quadragesimae tempore, pueros sic instituere ut sancte Sancta primum de altari libent.

[37] Cappello, *De Sacramentis,* I, 343.

[38] Canon 940.

In protracted diseases like tuberculosis, cancer, and similar disorders a disease endangering life is present, and therefore the patient is entitled to the reception of extreme unction. It happens often that the patient lives a long time before the disease finally takes him away. If the patient has rallied after the reception of extreme unction, but then again falls into the danger of death, he should be anointed again. At times it is difficult to know whether one crisis has completely passed and a new crisis has arisen, or whether there is a persistence of the same lingering condition caused by the same disease. If in protracted diseases the patient has recovered and feels considerably better for quite a while, about one month, moralists are of the opinion that the sick person may be anointed again. Pope Benedict XIV (1740-1758) taught that in a doubt whether the same danger continues or a new crisis has arisen, one should decide in favor of repetition of the sacrament, since a repetition in that case is more in conformity with the ancient practice of the Church.[39]

Extreme unction is to be given conditionally: (1) in doubt about the existence of the use of reason; (2) in doubt about the reality of the danger of death from an ailment; (3) in doubt about the fact that death itself has overtaken the person before the priest comes to anoint him; (4) in doubt about the continued status of impenitence. The sacrament is not to be administered to those who have obstinately and impenitently persevered in open mortal sin.[40] In all conditional anointings the form is, *Si capax es;* however, in cases wherein there is doubt whether death has overtaken the person before the priest comes to anoint him, the form should be, *Si vivis.*

Sick persons who, while they were still conscious, asked for the sacrament at least implicitly, or in all likelihood would have asked for it, are to be anointed absolutely though at the time they have lost consciousness or the use of reason.[41]

---

[39] Benedictus XIV, *De Synodo Dioecesana* (4 vols., Mechliniae, 1842), Lib. VIII, cap. 8, n. 4—II, 199-200; Kilker, *Extreme Unction*, pp. 123-202.

[40] Cf. canons 941-942; Woywod, *A Practical Commentary on the Code of Canon Law*, I, 478-481.

[41] Cf. canon 943; Woywod, *loc. cit.;* Kilker, *Extreme Unction*, 251-261.

Though this sacrament is not in itself necessary as a means of salvation, no one is accorded the freedom to neglect receiving it. Great care and solicitude must be used in order to have the sick person receive extreme unction while he is fully conscious.[42]

In regard to excommunicated persons as well as those who are personally interdicted, the last sacraments cannot be administered to them as long as their contumacy remains. However, once their contumacy has been broken, then any priest can absolve them from any penalty or censure when they are in danger of death, and thereupon Holy Viaticum and extreme unction should be administered to them. The minister must employ all necessary means for the precluding of possible scandal and for the obviating of whatever scandal may have emerged.

The administration of the last sacraments to dying non-Catholics is not discussed in this dissertation. Such a discussion would prove unduly lengthy, and furthermore it relates to the subject or the recipient rather than to the minister of the last sacraments.[43]

ARTICLE 2. THE GRANTING OF THE APOSTOLIC BLESSING WITH A PLENARY INDULGENCE AT THE MOMENT OF DEATH

The Code orders that the apostolic blessing with the plenary indulgence should be imparted to the dying person by the pastor or by some other officiating priest.[44] The apostolic blessing should be imparted to the dying person after his confession has been heard and after Viaticum and extreme unction respectively have been administered.[45]

This form of general absolution can be given to those who are in serious danger of death from any cause whatsoever; but the indulgence of the absolution itself remains suspended and is not effected until the actual moment preceding death. Consequently

---

[42] Cf. canon 944.

[43] Cf. King, *The Administration of the Sacraments to Dying Non-Catholics,* The Catholic University of America Canon Law Studies, n. 23 (Washington, D. C.: The Catholic University of America, 1924).

[44] Canon 468, § 2: Parocho aliive sacerdoti qui infirmis assistat, facultas est eis concedendi benedictionem apostolicam cum indulgentia plenaria in articulo mortis, secundum formam a probatis liturgicis libris traditam, quam benedictionem impertiri ne omittat.

[45] *Rituale Romanum,* Tit. V, cap. 6, n. 1.

this blessing cannot be repeated or granted again to a person who is afflicted with the same illness, regardless of how long that illness may last. This is true even if the stricken person has sinned mortally after the blessing had been given. The blessing may be given again, however, if the stricken person recovers, and afterwards has again become seriously ill.[46]

The formula as prescribed by Pope Benedict XIV is followed even today.[47]

The blessing should be imparted even to those who are destitute of their senses, as long as while having the full use of their senses they requested the blessing or gave some signs of sorrow for their sins. It can be imparted to those who have become delirious or insane. It should be denied, however, to excommunicates and impenitents as well as those who are dying in manifest mortal sin.

The stricken person should invoke the name of Jesus at least mentally, if he is conscious. During the imparting of the blessing all the sufferings and the illness itself which the person is undergoing should be offered to God in expiation for former sins. The person should express the wish that he willingly accepts death itself in satisfaction for the penalties resulting from the commission of his sins.[48]

ARTICLE 3. THE RIGHT OF PASTORS TO ADMINISTER CONFIRMATION IN VIRTUE OF THE APOSTOLIC INDULT OF SEPTEMBER 14, 1946

The Holy See has accorded to all territorial pastors the power to administer the sacrament of confirmation under certain conditions.[49] Only those parochial vicars are granted this faculty who are perpetual vicars of a filial church enjoying a permanent status; vicars econome and vicars of moral persons are granted this faculty too.[50] Priests belonging to a religious institute when

---

[46] Cf. Merkelbach, *Quaestiones Pastorales*, III, 107-108.

[47] Const. *Pia Mater*, 9 apr. 1747—*Fontes*, n. 380.

[48] *Rituale Romanum*, Tit. V, cap. 6, nn. 2-4.

[49] S. C. de Sacramentis, *Decretum*, 14 sept. 1946—*AAS*, XXXVIII (1946), 349-358.

[50] Bastnagel, "Parochial Vicars and the Faculty to Confer Confirmation," *The Jurist*, VII (1947), 174-178; Hannan, "Decrees and Decisions," *The Jurist*, VII (1947), 226-228.

given charge of a parish are vicars of the religious house or institute only when the religious house or institute is itself the pastor (*parochus*), and this is effected only by means of a complete union of the parish with the religious house or institute.[51] When such priests are appointed pastors of secular parishes, i.e., parishes not united *pleno iure* to a religious institute, then, though they are not vicars of the latter, they are nevertheless truly pastors; they also have the faculty of conferring confirmation.

Personal pastors are granted this faculty when they have charge of all the persons living in a definite territory, even though this territory is cumulatively subject to a territorial pastor. Pastors of national parishes are authorized by the present decree to confer the sacrament of confirmation. Military chaplains who are personal pastors to whom a definite territory has not been assigned cannot participate in this concession. The diocesan administrator and the vicar general are not included in this concession either, unless they are pastors. Assistants, chaplains of hospitals and other institutions, seminary rectors and superiors of religious houses are also excluded from participation in it.

This power cannot be subdelegated, but must be used personally. The pastor may validly and licitly confer the sacrament on any member of the faithful within the parish limits regardless of whether or not the person is his subject.

The person to be confirmed must be in serious danger of death by reason of grave illness. If the danger arises from an extrinsic cause, such as the imminence of battle in the case of a soldier, electrocution in the case of a condemned man, or an air raid in the case of a civilian, the use of the faculty is not justified. Hannan suggests that in practice those possessing the faculty of conferring the sacrament would be justified in using it if they can make a decision that the time has come for the administration of extreme unction.[52]

A condition insisted on by the decree is that the pastor may not use this faculty if a bishop, even a titular bishop, is available. There appears to be a discussion whether the administration of

---

[51] Cf. cc. 452, §§ 1, 2; 1423, § 2; 1425, § 2.

[52] Hannan, "Decisions and Decrees,"—*The Jurist*, VII (1947), 228-229.

the sacrament by the pastor would be invalid or illicit if a bishop would be available at the time of the administration. The word "*dummodo*" used in the decree specifying the unavailability of a bishop as a condition to be fulfilled before the faculty can be used might argue for the condition affecting the validity of the administration.[53] Hannan, however, points out that canon 39 sets forth a rule of interpretation for rescripts, not for laws enacted "*ex certa scientia*."[54] The author believes that the availability or unavailability of the bishop affects not the validity but the licitness of the pastor's administration of the sacrament.

This faculty extends to the confirmation of adults and infants. Persons who are insane, idiots, etc., even from birth are included under the classification of infants.

The pastor in administering the sacrament should instruct the dying person in keeping with his intelligence and he should stimulate in him a desire for the reception of the sacrament, if the person is conscious and in possession of the use of his reason.

The Holy See has granted the chaplains of maternity hospitals the power to administer the sacrament of confirmation to those infants who are in serious danger of death. The chaplain must be permanently appointed to the maternity hospital and he must administer the sacrament personally. If more than one chaplain is present at the hospital, then the first or senior member must administer the sacrament. Before the chaplain may use this faculty licitly, he must be morally certain that no bishop, residential or titular, is available for the administration either because of absence from the diocese or because of other impending duties. Furthermore, the chaplain must ascertain that the local pastor is unavailable for the administration because of absence from his parish or other pressing duties. In the absence of the chaplain, of the bishop, and of the local pastor no other priest may validly confer this sacrament to the infants.

It is to be noted that the rescript was made effective for only

[53] Cf. can. 39: "Conditiones in rescriptis tunc tantum essentiales pro eorum validitate censentur cum per particulas *si*, *dummodo*, vel aliam eiusdem significationem exprimuntur."

[54] Cf. Decisions and Decrees,"—*The Jurist*, VII (1947), 229.

one year, computed from October 26, 1948.[55] However, the faculty has been extended for another year, computed from February 6, 1950.[56]

ARTICLE 4. THE RITE IN WHICH THE LAST SACRAMENTS ARE ADMINISTERED

The Code enacts the general rule that in the administration and reception of all the sacraments everyone must follow his own rite.[57] Thus, for last confession a Latin priest should absolve a Latin penitent according to the Latin form of absolution, and an Oriental priest should absolve an Oriental penitent according to the Oriental form of absolution. However, in a case of emergency or urgent necessity, any priest of any rite could absolve a person of any rite, and the form of absolution would be given in accordance with the proper form of the priest's proper rite.

Holy Viaticum must be received in one's own rite; however, in urgent necessity the stricken person may receive the Holy Eucharist in any rite.[58] Regarding the case of necessity the Code states that in circumstances when the ministering priest is not of the same rite as the stricken person it is permissible for the Oriental priest to use unleavened bread instead of the leavened bread which he ordinarily uses, and the Latin priest may use leavened bread instead of the unleavened bread which he is wont to use. The rites and ceremonies, however, of the minister's proper rite must be adhered to in the actual administration.[59]

Although the Code does not explicitly state that in a case of necessity the sacrament of extreme unction may be administered in a rite other than the rite of the stricken person, nevertheless, by analogy with the rulings regarding the administration of the sacraments of last confession and Viaticum, a priest or priests of a different rite than that of the stricken person could and should administer extreme unction in a case of necessity. The

---

[55] Cf. "Decrees and Decisions,"—*The Jurist,* IX (1949), 261-262.

[56] Cf. "Decrees and Decisions,"—*The Jurist,* X (1950), 214.

[57] Canon 733, § 2.

[58] Canon 866, § 2.

[59] Canon 851, § 2.

minister would observe the rites and ceremonies of his own proper rite in the administration of the sacrament.

It should be noted that by no means does the reception of the last sacraments in a rite other than the proper rite of the sick person effect any change of rite for the latter.

ARTICLE 5. THE MANNER OF PROCEDURE AGAINST A PASTOR NEGLIGENT IN THE FULFILLMENT OF HIS PASTORAL DUTIES

If a pastor grossly neglects or violates the pastoral duties of administering the sacraments and of assisting the sick and the dying, the bishop shall admonish him, reminding him of his strict obligation in conscience, and of the penalties which the law decrees against these offenses.[60]

If the pastor does not amend, and if the bishop, after having consulted two of the diocesan examiners and given the pastor an opportunity to defend himself, has found proof that the parochial duties have repeatedly been neglected or violated for a notable length of time without any just excuse, he shall rebuke the pastor, and impose on him an appropriate penalty in proportion to his guilt.[61]

If both the rebuke and the punishment prove unavailing, the ordinary, after having proved according to canon 2183 the pastor's culpable perseverance in the neglect or violation of the pastoral duties, may at once deprive a removable pastor of his parish; he may deprive an irremovable pastor of the income of his benefice, either in whole or in part in proportion to the gravity of his guilt, and distribute it among the poor.[62] If the contumacy of the irremovable pastor continues and is proved in the manner described above, the ordinary can remove even an irremovable pastor from his parish.[63]

Recourse to the Holy See against the final decree of removal is governed by canon 2146. Such a recourse remains without any

---

[60] Cf. canon 2182.
[61] Cf. canon 2183.
[62] Cf. canon 2184.
[63] Cf. canon 2185.

suspensive effect against the issued decree until the higher authority has decided otherwise.

In regard to the administration of confirmation the Code states that a priest who neither by law nor by concession of the Roman Pontiff has the faculty to administer the sacrament of confirmation, and yet dares to administer this sacrament, shall be suspended. A priest who presumes to administer confirmation beyond the limits of the faculty conceded to him, particularly the faculty just recently conceded to territorial pastors, is automatically deprived of the faculty.[64]

[64] Cf. canon 2365.

CONCLUSIONS

1. It is the first conclusion of the writer that the Church through its conciliar laws, whether general or particular, from the earliest centuries granted to its faithful at the moment of death the privilege to confess to any priest and to receive absolution from all sins. The Council of Trent in legislating for the entire Church formulated a general decree to this effect. And the Code merely incorporated the decree of the Council into its own legislation.

2. The administration of the last sacraments by the local pastor as one of his many parochial rights and obligations was recognized by writers even before the Council of Trent. Pre-Code canonists particularly emphasized this particular right of the local pastor. The Code itself recognized and incorporated this long-standing right and obligation into its canons.

3. The law does not make any explicit provision for the administration of the last sacraments to the pastor himself. Canon 447, § 3, however, points very definitely to the dean as having in this matter a responsibility for the pastors in his deanery.

4. As a reserved parochial function, the administration of Holy Viaticum is restricted to that Communion which is prescribed by divine as well as ecclesiastical law when one falls into serious danger of death; it does not extend to other Communions which by way of Viaticum one receives out of devotion while seriously ill.

5. The pastor of a national parish is restricted in his administration of the last sacraments to those persons who, being members of that particular nationality and residing within the territorial limits of the parish, have of their own volition joined his parish. If the pastor of a national parish is unable or fails to administer the sacraments, then the local pastor of the territorial parish is obliged to administer those sacraments. On the contrary, the pastor of the national parish does not have the parochial obligation of assisting those whom the territorial pastor is unable or fails to assist, namely, his own parishioners who are within the

territorial limits of the parish, and also all others who are within the parish limits, except those who are exempted by the Code, as the religious, the seminarians, etc.

6. Although Holy Viaticum can be administered and the concession contained in canon 882 becomes applicable whenever a person is in danger of death from any cause, yet the sacrament of extreme unction can be administered solely to those who are in danger of death from illness or old age. Thus a criminal condemned to die could receive Holy Viaticum, and he could avail himself of the privilege granted by canon 882, but he could not receive extreme unction.

7. The current practice in this country of not having a cleric or a lay person accompanying the priest on a sick-call is warranted by present-day circumstances.

8. The current practice, however, of not wearing a cassock, a surplice, and a stole in the sick room during the administration of the Eucharist to the sick according to the requirements of the *Roman Ritual* is not considered a reasonable and legitimate practice in view of present-day circumstances.

BIBLIOGRAPHY

Sources

Acta Apostolicae Sedis, Commentarium Officiale, Romae, 1909-

Acta Sanctae Sedis, 41 vols., Romae, 1865-1908.

Bouscaren, T. Lincoln, *The Canon Law Digest,* 2 vols., Milwaukee: Bruce, 1934, 1943.

Bruns, Hermann T., *Canones Apostolorum et Conciliorum Saeculorum IV-VII,* 2 vols., Berolini, 1839.

Bullarum Diplomatum et Privilegiorum Sanctorum Pontificum Taurinensis Editio, 24 vols. et Appendix, Augustae Taurinorum, 1857-1872.

Catechismus ex Decreto Concilii Tridentini ad Parochos Pii V Pontificis Max., et deinde Clementis XIII, Iussu Editus, Taurini-Romae: Marietti, 1930.

Codex Iuris Canonici Pii X Pontificis Maximi iussu digestus Benedicti Papae XV auctoritate promulgatus, Romae: Typis Polyglottis Vaticanis, 1917. Reimpressio, 1932.

Codicis Iuris Canonici Fontes, cura Emi Petri Card. Gasparri editi, 9 vols., Romae (later Civitate Vaticana): Typis Polyglottis Vaticanis, 1923-1939. (Vols. VII-IX, ed. cura et studio Emi Iustiniani Card. Serédi.)

Collectanea in Usum Secretariae Sacrae Congregationis Episcoporum et Regularium, cura A. Bizzarri, secretarii, Romae, 1885.

Collectanea S. Congregationis de Propaganda Fide, 2 vols., Romae: Typographia Polyglotta, S. C. de Propaganda Fide, 1907.

Concilii Plenarii Baltimorensis II Acta et Decreta, Baltimorae: John Murphy, 1868.

Corpus Iuris Canonici, Editio Lipsiensis II (Richter-Friedberg), 2 vols., Lipsiae, 1879-1881.

Corpus Scriptorum Ecclesiasticorum Latinorum, 72 vols., Vindobonae: F. Tempsky, 1866-

Decreta Authentica Congregationis Sacrorum Rituum ex Actis eiusdem collecta eiusque auctoritate promulgata sub Auspiciis SS. D. N. Leonis Papae XIII, 5 vols. et 2 Appendices, Romae: Typis Polyglottis Vaticanis, 1898-1927.

Decretales D. Gregorii Papae IX, suae integritati, una cum glossis restituta, Romae, 1582.

Denzinger, H.-Bannwart, C.-Umberg, J., *Enchiridion Symbolorum Definitionum et Declarationum de Rebus Fidei et Morum,* 21.-23. ed., St. Louis: Herder and Co., 1937.

Hardouin, Jean, *Acta Conciliorum et Epistolae Decretales ac Constitutiones Summorum Pontificum,* 12 vols., Parisiis, 1714-1715.

Hefele, Carolus-Leclerq, Henricus, *Histoire des Conciles*, 10 vols. in 19, Paris: Letouzey et Ané, 1907-1938.

Jaffé, Phillipus, *Regesta Pontificum Romanorum ab condita Ecclesia ad annum post Christum natum MCXCVIII*, 2. ed., cura G. Wattenbach, F. Kaltenbrunner (ad annum 590), P. Ewald (anno 590-882), S. Lowenfeld (anno 882-1198), 2 vols. in 1, Lipsiae, 1885-1888.

Mansi, J. D., *Sacrorum Conciliorum Nova et Amplissima Collectio*, 53 vols. in 60, Parisiis, 1901-1927.

Monumenta Germaniae Historica, 188 vols., incomplete, Hannoverae, 1826-; Leges in 4°, Sectio III (*Concilia*) Tom. II, ed. A. Werminghoff, 1906-1908.

Pallottini, Salvator, *Collectio omnium conclusionum et resolutionum quae in causis propositis apud Sacram Congregationem Cardinalium S. Concilii Tridentini Interpretum prodierunt ab eius institutione anno MDLXIV ad annum MDCCCLX, distinctis titulis alphabetico ordine per materias digestas*, 17 vols., Romae, 1868-1893.

Potthast, A., *Regesta Pontificum Romanorum inde ab anno post Christum natum MCXCVIII ad annum MCCCIV*, 2 vols., Berolini, 1874-1875.

Rituale Romanum, Editio juxta Typicam Vaticanam, Neo Eboraci: Benziger Brothers, 1944.

Schroeder, H. J., *Canons and Decrees of the Council of Trent*, St. Louis: Herder, 1941.

Thesaurus Resolutionum Sacrae Congregationis Concilii, 167 vols., Romae, 1718-1908.

Wilkins, David, *Concilia Magnae Brittaniae et Hiberniae a Synodo Verolamiensi A. D. 446 ad Londonensem A. D. 1717*, 4 vols., London, 1737.

Authors

Acta Sanctorum, editio novissima curante Ioanne Carnandet, Parisiis et Romae, 1863-1870.

Aertnys, A.-Damen, C. A., *Theologia Moralis*, 13. ed., 2 vols., Taurini-Romae: Marietti, 1939.

André, M.-Wagner, J., *Dictionnaire de Droit Canonique*, 5. ed., 4 vols., Paris, 1901.

Aquinas, St. Thomas, *Sancti Thomae Aquinatis Commentum in Quatuor Libros Sententiarum*, 2 vols., Parmae, 1858.

Augustine, Charles, *A Commentary on the New Code of Canon Law*, 8 vols., Vol. II, 3. ed., 1919; Vol. III, 2. ed., 1919; Vol. IV, 2. ed., 1920; Vol. V, 2. rev. ed., 1920; Vol. VI, 3. ed., 1931, St. Louis: Herder & Co.

Ballerini, A., *Opus Theologicum Morale*, absolvit et editit Dominicus Palmieri, 7 vols., Prati, 1889-1893.

Barbosa, A., *De Officio et Potestate Parochi Descriptio*, ed. U. Giraldi a S. Cajetano, Romae, 1774.

Benedictus XIV, *De Synodo Dioecesana*, 4 vols., Mechliniae, 1842.

Bernardus Papiensis, *Summa Decretalium,* ed. E. A. T. Laspeyres, Ratisbonae, 1860.

Beste, Udalricus, *Introductio in Codicem,* 3. ed., Collegeville, St. John's Abbey Press, 1946.

Blat, Albertus, *Commentarium Textus Iuris Canonici,* 5 vols. in 6, Romae: Ex Typographia Pontificia in Instituto Pii IX, Vol. II, 2. ed., 1921; Vol. III, Pars I, 2. ed., 1924; Vol. III, Pars II, 1923.

Bord, J. B., *L'Extreme Onction,* Bruges, 1923.

Bouix, Dominicus, *Tractatus de Parocho,* 3. ed., Parisiis, 1880.

Cabrol, F.-Leclerq, H., *Monumenta Ecclesiae Liturgica,* 6 vols., Parisiis, 1900-1902.

Callan, C. and McHugh, J., *Catechism of the Council of Trent for Parish Priests,* Seventh Printing, New York: Wagner, 1943.

Cappello, F. M., *Summa Iuris Canonici,* 3 vols., Vol. II, 4. ed., Romae: Apud Aedes Universitatis Gregorianae, 1945.

———, *Tractatus Canonico-Moralis de Sacramentis,* 3 vols. in 6, Romae: Domus Editorialis Marietti, 1935-1945; Vol. I, 4. ed., 1945; Vol. II, pars I, 4. ed., 1944; Vol. II, pars II, 2. ed., 1942; Vol. II, pars III, 1935; Vol. III, partes I, II, 4. ed., 1939.

———, *De Censuris iuxta Codicem Iuris Canonici,* Augustae Taurinorum: Marietti, 1919.

Catalanus, Jos., *Rituale Romanum Benedicti Papae XII Jussu Editum,* 2 vols., Patavii, 1760.

Cerato, P., *Censurae Vigentes Ipso Facto a Codice Iuris Canonici Excerptae,* 2. ed., Patavii, 1921.

Chardon, C., *Histoire des Sacrements—MTC,* XX, 11-1152.

Ciesluk, J., *National Parishes in the United States,* The Catholic University of America Canon Law Studies, n. 190, Washington, D. C.: The Catholic University of America Press, 1944.

Cocchi, G., *Commentarium in Codicem Iuris Canonici,* 8 vols., Vol. IV, 3. ed., Augustae Taurinorum: Marietti, 1932.

Conran, Edward, *The Interdict,* The Catholic University of America Canon Law Studies, n. 56, Washington, D. C.: The Catholic University of America Press, 1930.

Corluy, Josephus, *Specilegium Dogmatico-Biblicum,* 3 vols., Gandavi, 1884.

Coronata, Matthaeus Conte a, *De Locis et Temporibus Sacris,* Augustae Taurinorum: Marietti, 1922.

———, *Institutiones Iuris Canonici ad usum utriusque cleri et scholarum,* 2. ed., 5 vols., Taurini: Marietti, 1939-1947.

———, *Institutiones Iuris Canonici ad usum utriusque cleri et scholarum "De Sacramentis,"* 3 vols., Romae: Marietti, 1943-1946.

Crotty, Matthew, *The Recipient of First Holy Communion,* The Catholic University of America Canon Law Studies, n. 247, Washington, D. C.: The Catholic University of America Press, 1947.

Curci, Carlo M., *Il Nuovo Testamento,* 3 vols., Romae, 1880.

Davis, H., *Moral and Pastoral Theology,* 4. ed., 4 vols., London, New York: Sheed and Ward, 1943.

De Augustinis, Aegidius, *De Re Sacramentaria,* 4 vols. in 2, Woodstock, Maryland, 1878.

De Luca, Ioannes B., *Theatrum Veritatis et Iustitiae,* 16 vols. in 4, Romae, 1706.

De Lugo, Ioannes, *Disputationes Scholasticae et Morales,* ed. nova, 8 vols., Parisiis: apud Ludovicum Vivés, 1868-1869.

De Meester, A., *Juris Canonici et Juris Canonico-Civilis Compendium,* nova editio, 3 vols. in 4, Brugis: Desclée, De Brouwer et Sii, 1921-1928.

Denzinger, H., *Ritus Orientalium, Coptorum, Syrorum et Armenorum in Administrandis Sacramentorum,* 2 vols., Wirceburgi, 1863.

Dictionnaire de Théologie Catholique, 14 vols. in 23, Paris, 1903-1939.

Drumm, William, *Hospital Chaplains,* The Catholic University of America Canon Law Studies, n. 178, Washington, D. C.: The Catholic University of America Press, 1943.

Durantis, G., *Rationale Divinorum Officiorum,* Neapoli, 1859.

Fanfani, L., *De Iure Parochorum ad Normam Codicis Iuris Canonici,* Romae: Marietti, 1924.

———, *De Iure Religiosorum ad Normam Codicis Iuris Canonici,* 2. ed., Taurini: Marietti, 1924.

Ferraris, Lucius, *F. Lucii Ferraris Promptae Bibliothecae Supplementum,* ed. a Ianuario Bucceroni, Romae, 1899.

Ferreres, Ioannes, *Compendium Theologiae Moralis,* 14. ed., 2 vols., Barcinone, 1928.

———, *Institutiones Canonicae,* 2. ed., 2 vols., Barcinone, 1920.

Frank, F., *Die Bussdisciplin in der Kirche von den Apostelzeiten bis zum siebenten Jahrhundert,* Mainz, 1867.

Gasparri, Petrus, *De Sanctissima Eucharistia,* 2 vols., Parisiis et Lugduni, 1897.

———, *De Sacra Ordinatione,* 2 vols., Parisiis, 1893.

Genicot, E.-Salsmans, I., *Institutiones Theologiae Moralis,* 11. ed., 2 vols., Bruxellis: Dewit, 1927.

Guilfoyle, Merlin, *Custom,* The Catholic University of America Canon Law Studies, n. 105, Washington, D. C.: The Catholic University of America, 1937.

Gury, J. P.-Ferreres, I., *Casus Conscientiae,* 2 vols., Barcinone, 1921.

Hostiensis, Cardinalis (Henricus de Segusia), *Summa Aurea,* Luduni, 1568.

Hurter, Hugo, *Theologiae Dogmaticae Compendium,* 12. ed., 3 vols., Oenitponte, 1909.

Jorio, D., *La Comunione agl' Infermi,* Romae: Pustet, 1931.

Kelly, James, *The Jurisdiction of the Simple Confessor,* The Catholic University of America Canon Law Studies, n. 43, Washington, D. C.: The Catholic University of America, 1927.

Kern, J., *De Sacramento Extremae Unctionis Tractatus Dogmaticus,* Ratisbonae, 1907.

Kilker, Adrian, *Extreme Unction,* The Catholic University of America Canon Law Studies, n. 32, Washington, D. C.: The Catholic University of America, 1926.

King, James, *The Administration of the Sacraments to Dying Non-Catholics,* The Catholic University of America Canon Law Studies, n. 23, Washington, D. C.: The Catholic University of America, 1924.

Kurtscheid, B.-Wilches, F., *Historia Iuris Canonici,* 2 vols., Romae: Officium Libri Catholici, 1941-1943.

Laurain, Paul, *De l'intervention des laiques, des diacres et des abbesses dans l'administration de la penitence,* Paris, 1897.

Laymann, P., *Theologia Moralis,* 2 vols., Patavii, 1783.

Lehmkuhl, A., *Theologia Moralis,* 14. ed., 2 vols., Friburgi Brisgoviae, 1914.

Lexicon Biblicum, 3 vols., ed. a M. Hagen, Paris, 1911, in *Cursus Scripturae Sacrae* (auctoribus R. Cornely, J. Knabenbauer, F. Hummelauer).

Liguori, St. Alphonsus, *Theologia Moralis,* 3 vols., Augustae Taurinorum, 1891.

Marc, C.-Gestermann, F., *Institutiones Morales Alphonsianae,* 18. ed., 2 vols., Lugduni et Lutetiae Parisiorum, 1927.

Martène, Edmundus, *De Antiquis Ecclesiae Ritibus,* 4 vols., Rouen, 1700-1706.

Maschat, Remigius a S. Erasmo, *Institutiones Canonicae,* 4 vols. in 2, Florentiae, 1854.

McCormick, Robert, *Confessors of Religious,* The Catholic University of America Canon Law Studies, n. 33, Washington, D. C.: The Catholic University of America, 1926.

Ménard, Hugo, *Notae in S. Gregorii Librum Sacramentorum, Auctore D. Hugone Menardo, Monacho Benedictino—MPL,* LXXVIII, 263-582.

Merkelbach, Ben. H., *Quaestiones Pastorales,* 6 vols., Liege, 1927-1930.

Migne, J. P., *Patrologiae Cursus Completus, Series Latina,* 221 vols., Parisiis, 1844-1864.

———, *Series Graeca,* 161 vols., Parisiis, 1856-1866.

———, *Theologiae Cursus Completus,* 28 vols., Parisiis, 1839-1845.

Moriarty, Francis, *The Extraordinary Absolution from Censures,* The Catholic University of America Canon Law Studies, n. 113, Washington, D. C.: The Catholic University of America, 1938.

Morinus, J., *Commentarius Historicus de Disciplina in Administratione Sacramenti Poenitentiae,* Antverpiae, 1682.

Noldin, H.-Schmitt, A., *Summa Theologiae Moralis iuxta Codicem Iuris Canonici,* 26. ed., 3 vols., Oeniponte/Lipsiae: Felician Rauch, 1940.

O'Kane, J.-Fallon, M. J., *Notes on the Rubrics of the Roman Ritual,* 4. ed., Dublin: Duffy, 1938.

Pehem, J., *Ius Ecclesiasticum Universum,* 2 vols., Viennae, 1785.

Pennafort, St. Raymond, *Summa,* Veronae, 1744.

Petavius, Dionysius, *Dogmata-Theologica,* ed. J. B. Fournials, 8 vols., Parisiis, 1866-1868.

Pirhing, Ernricus, *Ius Canonicum Nova Methodo Explicatum,* 5 vols., Dilingae, 1674-1678.

Piscetta, A.-Gennaro, A., *Elementa Theologiae Moralis,* 7 vols., Vol. V, 6. ed., Torino: Societá Editrice Internazionale, 1946.

Pohle, J.-Preuss, A., *The Sacraments,* 3. rev. ed., 4 vols., St. Louis: 1919-1920.

Prümmer, D., *Manuale Theologiae Moralis,* 3. ed., 3 vols., Friburgi Brisgoviae, 1923.

Rainer, Eligius, *Suspension of Clerics,* The Catholic University of America Canon Law Studies, n. 111, Washington, D. C.: The Catholic University of America, 1937.

Regatillo, E., *Ius Sacramentarium,* 2 vols., Santander: Sal Terrae, 1945-1946.

Schell, Hermann, *Katholische Dogmatik,* 4 vols., Paderborn, 1889-1893.

Schmalzgrueber, F., *Ius Ecclesiasticum Universum,* 5 vols. in 12, Romae, 1843-1845.

Schroeder, H. J., *Disciplinary Decrees of the General Councils, Text, Translation and Commentary,* St. Louis, Herder, 1937.

Sole, J., *De Delictis et Poenis,* Romae, 1920.

Suarez, Franciscus, *Opera Omnia,* 28 vols., Parisiis, 1856-1861.

Tanquerey, A., *Synopsis Theologiae Dogmaticae,* 24. ed., 3 vols., Parisiis: Desclée et Socii, 1938.

Teetaert, A., *La Confession aux Laiques dans l'Eglise Latine depuis le VIIIe Siécle jusqu'au XIVe,* Paris, 1926.

Van Espen, Z. B., *Compendium Iuris Ecclesiastici,* 2 vols., Bassani, 1784.

Van Hove, A., *Commentarium Lovaniense in Codicem Iuris Canonici,* Vol. I, tom. 1, *Prolegomena ad Codicem Iuris Canonici,* 2. ed., Mechliniae et Romae: Dessain, 1945.

Vermeersch, A., *Theologia Moralis,* 3. ed., 4 vols., Romae: Universita Gregoriana, 1933-1937.

Vermeersch, A.-Creusen, J., *Epitome Iuris Canonici,* 3 vols., Vol. I, 6. ed., Mechliniae: Dessain, 1937; Vol. II, 2. ed., Bruxellis et Brugis, 1925.

Waldron, Joseph, *The Minister of Baptism,* The Catholic University of America Canon Law Studies, n. 170, Washington, D. C.: The Catholic University of America Press, 1942.

Wernz, F. X., *Ius Decretalium,* 2. ed., 6 vols., Romae et Prati, 1906-1913.

Wernz, F. X.-Vidal, P., *Ius Canonicum ad Codicis Normam Exactum,* 7 vols. in 8, Vol. IV, pars I, Romae: Apud Aedes Universitatis Gregorianae, 1934.

Woywod, S., *A Practical Commentary on the Code of Canon Law,* 2 vols., Tenth Printing, New York: Joseph F. Wagner, 1946.

Zitelli, Zephyrinus, *Apparatus Iuris Ecclesiastici,* Romae, 1888.

Articles

Bastnagel, C., "Parochial Vicars and the Faculty to Confer Confirmation," *The Jurist,* VII (1947), 174-178.

———, "Parish Assistants and the Prenuptial Investigation," *The Jurist*, VII (1947), 171-174.

Hannan, J., "Decrees and Decisions," *The Jurist*, VII (1947), 226-233.

Jone, H., "Die Absolutionsvollmachten in Todesgefahr," *Theologische-praktische Quartalschift*, LXXIX (1926), 12-21, 237-250.

Kelly, J., "Faculties of Absolving and Dispensing in Danger of Death," *The Ecclesiastical Review*, LXXXV (1931), 255-257.

McNicholas, J. T., "The Age of Children for First Communion," *The Ecclesiastical Review*, XLIII (1910), 485.

Vermeersch, A., "De Exemptione Seminariorum," *Jus Pontificium*, I-II (1921-1922), 70.

Woywod, S., "The Legislation of the Code on Baptism," *The Homiletic and Pastoral Review*, XX (1920), 1037-1042.

Periodicals

American Ecclesiastical Review, The, Vols. I-XXXII, Philadelphia, 1895-1905; from 1905: *The Ecclesiastical Review*, Vols. XXXIII-CIX, Philadelphia, 1905-1943; from 1944: *The American Ecclesiastical Review*, Washington, D. C.

Homiletic and Pastoral Review, The, New York, 1900-

Jurist, The, Washington, D. C., 1941-

Jus Pontificium, Romae, 1921-1940.

Theologische-praktische Quartalschift, Linz, 1848-

ABBREVIATIONS

AAS—*Acta Apostolicae Sedis*
ASS—*Acta Sanctae Sedis*
Bizzarri—*Collectanea in Usum Secretariae Sacrae Congregationis Episcoporum et Regularium, cura A. Bizzarri, secretarii*
Bruns—*Canones Apostolorum et Conciliorum saec. IV-VII*, ed. Bruns.
Bull. Rom.—*Bullarum Diplomatum et Privilegiorum Sanctorum Pontificum Taurinensis Editio*
CSEL—*Corpus Scriptorum Ecclesiasticorum Latinorum*
Decr. Auth.—*Decreta Authentica Congregationis Sacrorum Rituum*
DTC—*Dictionnaire de Théologie Catholique*
Fontes—*Codicis Iuris Canonici Fontes*, cura . . . Gasparri editi
Hardouin—*Acta Conciliorum etc.*
Jaffé—*Regesta Pontificum Romanorum etc.*
Mansi—*Sacrorum Conciliorum Nova et Amplissima Collectio*
MGH—*Monumenta Germaniae Historica*
MPG—Migne, *Patrologia Graeca*
MPL—Migne, *Patrologia Latina*
MTC—Migne, *Theologiae Cursus Completus*
Pallottini—*Collectio omnium conclusionum et resolutionum etc.*
Potthast—*Regesta Pontificum Romanorum inde ab anno post Christum natum MCXCVIII ad annum MCCCIV*
S. C. C.—Sacra Congregatio Concilii
S. C. de Prop. Fide—Sacra Congregatio de Propaganda Fide
S. C. Ep. et Reg.—Sacra Congregatio Episcoporum et Regularium

BIOGRAPHICAL NOTE

Francis J. Statkus was born on September 17, 1921, in Philadelphia, Pennsylvania. He received his early education at St. Casimir's School and the Southeast Catholic High School for Boys. In 1937 he entered Saint Charles' Seminary, Overbrook, Pennsylvania, where he received the degree of Bachelor of Arts in 1943. He was ordained to the Sacred Priesthood on May 30, 1946. The following October he entered the Catholic University of America to pursue graduate studies in the School of Canon Law. He received the Baccalaureate in Canon Law in June, 1947, and the Licentiate in Canon Law in June, 1948.

ALPHABETICAL INDEX

CANON LAW STUDIES*

1. Freriks, Rev. Celestine A., C.PP.S., J.C.D., Religious Congregations in Their External Relations, 121 pp. 1916.
2. Galliher, Rev. Daniel M., O.P., J.C.D., Canonical Elections, 117 pp., 1917.
3. Borkowski, Rev. Aurelius L., O.F.M., J.C.D., De Confraternibus Ecclesiasticis, 136 pp., 1918.
4. Castillo, Rev. Cayo, J.C.D., Disertacion Historico-Canonica sobre la Potestad del Cabildo en Sede Vacante o Impedida del Vicario Capitular, 99 pp., 1919 (1918).
5. Kubelbeck, Rev. William J., S.T.B., J.C.D., The Sacred Penitentiaria and Its Relation to Faculties of Ordinaries and Priests, 129 pp., 1918.
6. Petrovits, Rev. Joseph, J.C., S.T.D., J.C.D., The New Church Law on Matrimony, X-461 pp., 1919.
7. Hickey, Rev. John J., S.T.B., J.C.D., Irregularities and Simple Impediments in the New Code of Canon Law, 100 pp., 1920.
8. Klekotka, Rev. Peter J., S.T.B., J.C.D., Diocesan Consultors, 179 pp., 1920.
9. Wanenmacher, Rev. Francis, J.C.D., The Evidence in Ecclesiastical Procedure Affecting the Marriage Bond, 1920 (Printed 1935).
10. Golden, Rev. Henry Francis, J.C.D., Parochial Benefices in the New Code, IV-119 pp., 1921 (Printed 1925).
11. Koudelka, Rev. Charles J., J.C.D., Pastors, Their Rights and Duties According to the New Code of Canon Law, 211 pp., 1921.
12. Melo, Rev. Antonius, O.F.M., J.C.D., De Exemptione Regularium, X-188 pp., 1921.
13. Schaaf, Rev. Valentine Theodore, O.F.M., S.T.B., J.C.D., The Cloister, X-180 pp., 1921.
14. Burke, Rev. Thomas Joseph, S.T.D., J.C.D., Competence in Ecclesiastical Tribunals, IV-117 pp., 1922.
15. Leech, Rev. George Leo, J.C.D., A Comparative Study of the Constitution "Apostolicae Sedis" and the "Codex Juris Canonici," 179 pp., 1922.
16. Motry, Rev. Hubert Louis, S.T.D., J.C.D., Diocesan Faculties According to the Code of Canon Law, II-167 pp., 1922.
17. Murphy, Rev. George Lawrence, J.C.D., Delinquencies and Penalties in the Administration and the Reception of the Sacraments, IV-121 pp., 1923.

*All published numbers are available from the Catholic University of America Press, 620 Michigan Avenue, N.E., Washington 17, D. C., except the following: Nos. 1-114 inclusive, 115, 118, 120, 122, 123, 136, 153, 162, 182 and 198. But the following numbers, now reissued, are obtainable from *The Jurist*, The Catholic University of America, Washington 17, D. C., namely: Nos. 5, 7, 11, 17, 18, 19, 26, 28, 30, 31, 34, 42, 44, 51, 52 and 61.

18. O'Reilly, Rev. John Anthony, S.T.B., J.C.D., Ecclesiastical Sepulture in the New Code of Canon Law, II-129 pp., 1923.
19. Michalicka, Rev. Wenceslas Cyrill, O.S.B., J.C.D., Judicial Procedure in Dismissal of Clerical Exempt Religious, 107 pp., 1923.
20. Dargin, Rev. Edward Vincent, S.T.B., J.C.D., Reserved Cases According to the Code of Canon Law, IV-103 pp., 1924.
21. Godfrey, Rev. John A., S.T.B., J.C.D., The Right of Patronage According to the Code of Canon Law, 153 pp., 1924.
22. Hagedorn, Rev. Francis Edward, J.C.D., General Legislation on Indulgences, II-154 pp., 1924.
23. King, Rev. James Ignatius, J.C.D., The Administration of the Sacraments to Dying Non-Catholics, V-141 pp., 1924.
24. Winslow, Rev. Francis Joseph, O.F.M., J.C.D., Vicars and Prefects Apostolic, IV-149 pp., 1924.
25. Correa, Rev. Jose Servelion, S.T.L., J.C.D., La Potestad Legislativa de la Iglesia Catolica, IV-127 pp., 1925.
26. Dugan, Rev. Henry Francis, A.M., J.C.D., The Judiciary Department of the Diocesan Curia, 87 pp., 1925.
27. Keller, Rev. Charles Frederick, S.T.B., J.C.D., Mass Stipends, 167 pp., 1925.
28. Paschang, Rev. John Linus, J.C.D., The Sacramentals According to the Code of Canon Law, 129 pp., 1925.
29. Piontek, Rev. Cyrillus, O.F.M., S.T.B., J.C.D., De Indulto Exclaustrationis necnon Saecularizationis, XIII-289 pp., 1925.
30. Kearney, Rev. Richard Joseph, S.T.B., J.C.D., Sponsors at Baptism According to the Code of Canon Law, IV-127 pp., 1925.
31. Bartlett, Rev. Chester Joseph, A.M., LL.B., J.C.D., The Tenure of Parochial Property in the United States of America, V-108 pp., 1926.
32. Kilker, Rev. Adrian Jerome, J.C.D., Extreme Unction, V-425 pp., 1926.
33. McCormick, Rev. Robert Emmett, J.C.D., Confessors of Religious, VIII-266 pp., 1926.
34. Miller, Rev. Newton Thomas, J.C.D., Founded Masses According to the Code of Canon Law, VII-93 pp., 1926.
35. Roelker, Rev. Edward G., S.T.D., J.C.D., Principles of Privilege According to the Code of Canon Law, XI-166 pp., 1926.
36. Bakalarczyk, Rev. Richardus, M.I.C., J.U.D., De Novitiatu, VIII-208 pp., 1927.
37. Pizzuti, Rev. Lawrence, O.F.M., J.U.L., De Parochis Religiosis, 1927. (Not Printed.)
38. Bliley, Rev. Nicholas Martin, O.S.B., J.C.D., Altars According to the Code of Canon Law, XIX-132 pp., 1927.
39. Brown, Mr. Brendan Francis, A.B., LL.M., J.U.D., The Canonical Juristic Personality with Special Reference to its Status in the United States of America, V-212 pp., 1927.

40. Cavanaugh, Rev. William Thomas, C.P., J.U.D., The Reservation of the Blessed Sacrament, VIII-101 pp., 1927.
41. Doheny, Rev. William J., C.S.C., A.B., J.C.D., Church Property: Modes of Acquisition, X-118 pp., 1927.
42. Feldhaus, Rev. Aloysius H., C.PP.S., J.C.D., Oratories, IV-141 pp., 1927.
43. Kelly, Rev. James Patrick, A.B., J.C.D., The Jurisdiction of the Simple Confessor, X-208 pp., 1927.
44. Neuberger, Rev. Nicholas J., J.C.D., Canon 6 or the Relation of the Codex Iuris Canonici to the Preceding Legislation, V-95 pp., 1927.
45. O'Keefe, Rev. Gerald Michael, J.C.D., Matrimonial Dispensations, Powers of Bishops, Priests, and Confessors, VIII-232 pp., 1927.
46. Quigley, Rev. Joseph A. M., A.B., J.C.D., Condemned Societies, 139 pp., 1927.
47. Zaplotnik, Rev. Johannes Leo, J.C.D., De Vicariis Foraneis, X-142 pp., 1927.
48. Duskie, Rev. John Aloysius, A.B., J.C.D., The Canonical Status of the Orientals in the United States, VIII-196 pp., 1928.
49. Hyland, Rev. Francis Edward, J.C.D., Excommunication, Its Nature, Historical Development and Effects, VIII-181 pp., 1928.
50. Reimann, Rev. Gerald Joseph, O.M.C., J.C.D., The Third Order Secular of Saint Francis, 201 pp., 1928.
51. Schenk, Rev. Francis J., J.C.D., The Matrimonial Impediments of Mixed Religion and Disparity of Cult, XVI-318 pp., 1929.
52. Coady, Rev. John Joseph, S.T.D., J.U.D., A.M., The Appointment of Pastors, VIII-150 pp., 1929.
53. Kay, Rev. Thomas Henry, J.C.D., Competence in Matrimonial Procedure, VIII-164 pp., 1929.
54. Turner, Rev. Sidney Joseph, C.P., J.U.D., The Vow of Poverty, XLIX-217 pp., 1929.
55. Kearney, Rev. Raymond A., A.B., S.T.D., J.C.D., The Principles of Delegation, VII-149 pp., 1929.
56. Conran, Rev. Edward James, A.B., J.C.D., The Interdict, V-163 pp., 1930.
57. O'Neill, Rev. William H., J.C.D., Papal Rescripts of Favor, VII-218 pp., 1930.
58. Bastnagel, Rev. Clement Vincent, J.U.D., The Appointment of Parochial Adjutants and Assistants, XV-257 pp., 1930.
59. Ferry, Rev. William A., A.B., J.C.D., Stole Fees, V-136 pp., 1930.
60. Costello, Rev. John Michael, A.B., J.C.D., Domicile and Quasi-Domicile, VII-201 pp., 1930.
61. Kremer, Rev. Michael Nicholas, A.B., S.T.B., J.C.D., Church Support in the United States, VI-136 pp., 1930.
62. Angulo, Rev. Luis, C.M., J.C.D., Legislation de la Iglesia sobre la intencion en la application de la Santa Misa, VII-104 pp., 1931.

63. Frey, Rev. Wolfgang Norbert, O.S.B., A.B., J.C.D., The Act of Religious Profession, VIII-174 pp., 1931.
64. Roberts, Rev. James Brendan, A.B., J.C.D., The Banns of Marriage, XIV-140 pp., 1931.
65. Ryder, Rev. Raymond Aloysius, A.B., J.C.D., Simony, IX-151 pp., 1931.
66. Campagna, Rev. Angelo, Ph.D., J.U.D., Il Vicario Generale del Vescovo, VII-205, pp., 1931.
67. Cox, Rev. Joseph Godfrey, A.B., J.C.D., The Administration of Seminaries, VI-124 pp., 1931.
68. Gregory, Rev. Donald J., J.U.D., The Pauline Privilege, XV-165 pp., 1931.
69. Donohue, Rev. John F., J.C.D., The Impediment of Crime, VII-110 pp., 1931.
70. Dooley, Rev. Eugene A., O.M.I., J.C.D., Church Law on Sacred Relics, IX-143 pp., 1931.
71. Orth, Rev. Clement Raymond, O.M.C., J.C.D., The Approbation of Religious Institutes, 171 pp., 1931.
72. Pernicone, Rev. Joseph M., A.B., J.C.D., The Ecclesiastical Prohibition of Books, XII-267 pp., 1932.
73. Clinton, Rev. Connell, A.B., J.C.D., The Paschal Precept, IX-108 pp., 1932.
74. Donnelly, Rev. Francis B., A.M., S.T.L., J.C.D., The Diocesan Synod, VIII-125 pp., 1932.
75. Torrente, Rev. Camilo, C.M.F., J.C.D., Las Procesiones Sagradas, V-145 pp., 1932.
76. Murphy, Rev. Edwin J., C.PP.S., J.C.D., Suspension Ex Informata Conscientia, XI-122 pp., 1932.
77. MacKenzie, Rev. Eric F., A.M., S.T.L., J.C.D., The Delict of Heresy in its Commission, Penalization, Absolution, VII-124 pp., 1932.
78. Lyons, Rev. Avitus E., S.T.B., J.C.D., The Collegiate Tribunal of First Instance, XI-147 pp., 1932.
79. Connolly, Rev. Thomas A., J.C.D., Appeals, XI-195 pp., 1932.
80. Sangmeister, Rev. Joseph V., A.B., J.C.D., Force and Fear as Precluding Matrimonial Consent, V-211 pp., 1932.
81. Jaeger, Rev. Leo A., A.B., J.C.D., The Administration of Vacant and Quasi-Vacant Episcopal Sees in the United States, IX-229 pp., 1932.
82. Rimlinger, Rev. Herbert T., J.C.D., Error Invalidating Matrimonial Consent, VII-79 pp., 1932.
83. Barrett, Rev. John D. M., S.S., J.C.D., A Comparative Study of the Councils of Baltimore and the Code of Canon Law, IX-223 pp., 1932.
84. Carberry, Rev. John J., Ph.D., S.T.D., J.C.D., The Juridical Form of Marriage, X-177 pp., 1934.
85. Dolan, Rev. John L., A.B., J.C.D., The Defensor Vinculi, XII-157 pp., 1934.

86. HANNAN, REV. JEROME D., A.M., S.T.D., LL.B., J.C.D., The Canon Law of Wills, IX-517 pp., 1934.
87. LEMIEUX, REV. DELISE A., A.M., J.C.D., The Sentence in Ecclesiastical Procedure, IX-131 pp., 1934.
88. O'ROURKE, REV. JAMES J., A.B., J.C.D., Parish Registers, VII-109 pp., 1934.
89. TIMLIN, REV. BARTHOLOMEW, O.F.M., A.M., J.C.D., Conditional Matrimonial Consent, X-381 pp., 1934.
90. WAHL, REV. FRANCIS X., A.B., J.C.D., The Matrimonial Impediments of Consanguinity and Affinity, VI-125 pp., 1934.
91. WHITE, REV. ROBERT J., A.B., LL.B., S.T.B., J.C.D., Canonical Ante-Nuptial Promises and the Civil Law, VI-152 pp., 1934.
92. HERRERA, REV. ANTONIO PARRA, O.C.D., J.C.D., Legislacion Ecclesiastica sobra el Ayuno y la Abstinencia, XI-191 pp., 1935.
93. KENNEDY, REV. EDWIN J., J.C.D., The Special Matrimonial Process in Cases of Evident Nullity, X-165 pp., 1935.
94. MANNING, REV. JOHN J., A.B., J.C.D., Presumption of Law in Matrimonial Procedure, XI-111 pp., 1935.
95. MOEDER, REV. JOHN M., J.C.D., The Proper Bishop for Ordination and Dismissorial Letters, VII-135 pp., 1935.
96. O'MARA, REV. WILLIAM A., A.B., J.C.D., Canonical Causes for Matrimonial Dispensations, IX-155 pp., 1935.
97. REILLY, REV. PETER, J.C.D., Residence of Pastors, IX-81 pp., 1935.
98. SMITH, REV. MARINER T., O.P., S.T.Lr., J.C.D., The Penal Law for Religious, VIII-169 pp., 1935.
99. WHALEN, REV. DONALD W., A.M., J.C.D., The Value of Testimonial Evidence in Matrimonial Procedure, XIII-297 pp., 1935.
100. CLEARY, REV. JOSEPH F., J.C.D., Canonical Limitations on the Alienation of Church Property, VIII-141 pp., 1936.
101. GLYNN, REV. JOHN C., J.C.D., The Promoter of Justice, XX-337 pp., 1936.
102. BRENNAN, REV. JAMES H., S.S., M.A., S.T.B., J.C.D., The Simple Convalidation of Marriage, VI-135 pp., 1937.
103. BRUNINI, REV. JOSEPH BERNARD, J.C.D., The Clerical Obligations of Canons 139 and 142, X-121 pp., 1937.
104. CONNOR, REV. MAURICE, A.B., J.C.D., The Administrative Removal of Pastors, VIII-159 pp., 1937.
105. GUILFOYLE, REV. MERLIN JOSEPH, J.C.D., Custom, XI-144 pp., 1937.
106. HUGHES, REV. JAMES AUSTIN, A.B., A.M., J.C.D., Witnesses in Criminal Trials of Clerics, IX-140 pp., 1937.
107. JANSEN, REV. RAYMOND J., A.B., S.T.L., J.C.D., Canonical Provisions for Catechetical Instruction, VII-153 pp., 1937.
108. KEALY, REV. JOHN JAMES, A.B., J.C.D., The Introductory Libellus in Church Court Procedure, XI-121 pp., 1937.

109. McMANUS, REV. JAMES EDWARD, C.SS.R., J.C.D., The Administration of Temporal Goods in Religious Institutes, XVI-196 pp., 1937.
110. MORIARTY, REV. EUGENE JAMES, J.C.D., Oaths in Ecclesiastical Courts, X-115 pp., 1937.
111. RAINER, REG. ELIGIUS GEORGE, C.SS.R., J.C.D., Suspension of Clerics, XVII-249 pp., 1937.
112. REILLY, REV. THOMAS F., C.SS.R., J.C.D., Visitation of Religious, VI-195 pp., 1938.
113. MORIARTY, REV. FRANCIS E., C.SS.R., J.C.D., The Extraordinary Absolution from Censures, XV-334 pp., 1938.
114. CONNOLLY, REV. NICHOLAS P., J.C.D., The Canonical Erection of Parishes, X-132 pp., 1938.
115. DONOVAN, REV. JAMES JOSEPH, J.C.D., The Pastor's Obligation in Prenuptial Investigation, XII-322 pp., 1938.
116. HARRIGAN, REV. ROBERT J., M.A., S.T.B., J.C.D., The Radical Sanation of Invalid Marriages, VIII-208 pp., 1938.
117. BOFFA, REV. CONRAD HUMBERT, J.C.D., Canonical Provisions for Catholic Schools, VII-211 pp., 1939.
118. PARSONS, REV. ANSCAR JOHN, O.M.Cap., J.C.D., Canonical Elections, XII-236 pp., 1939.
119. REILLY, REV. EDWARD MICHAEL, A.B., J.C.D., The General Norms of Dispensation, XII-156 pp., 1939.
120. RYAN, REV. GERALD ALOYSIUS, A.B., J.C.D., Principles of Episcopal Jurisdiction, XII-172 pp., 1939.
121. BURTON, REV. FRANCIS JAMES, C.S.C., A.B., J.C.D., A Commentary on Canon 1125, X-222 pp., 1940.
122. MIASKIEWICZ, REV. FRANCIS SIGISMUND, J.C.D., Supplied Jurisdiction According to Canon 209, XII-340 pp., 1940.
123. RICE, REV. PATRICK WILLIAM, A.B., J.C.D., Proof of Death in Prenuptial Investigation, VIII-156 pp., 1940.
124. ANGLIN, REV. THOMAS FRANCIS, M.S., J.C.D., The Eucharistic Fast, VIII-183 pp., 1941.
125. COLEMAN, REV. JOHN JEROME, J.C.D., The Minister of Confirmation, VI-153 pp., 1941.
126. DOWNS, REV. JOHN EMMANUEL, A.B., J.C.D., The Concept of Clerical Immunity, XI-163 pp., 1941.
127. ESSWEIN, REV. ANTHONY ALBERT, J.C.D., Extrajudicial Penal Powers of Ecclesiastical Superiors, X-144 pp., 1941.
128. FARRELL, REV. BENJAMIN FRANCIS, M.A., S.T.L., J.C.D., The Rights and Duties of the Local Ordinary Regarding Congregations of Women Religious of Pontifical Approval, V-195 pp., 1941.
129. FEENEY, REV. THOMAS JOHN, A.B., S.T.L., J.C.D., Restitutio in Integrum, VI-169 pp., 1941.
130. FINDLAY, REV. STEPHEN WILLIAM, O.S.B., A.B., J.C.D., Canonical Norms Governing the Deposition and Degradation of Clerics, XVII-279 pp., 1941.

131. GOODWINE, REV. JOHN, A.B., S.T.L., J.C.D., The Right of the Church to Acquire Property, VIII-119 pp., 1941.
132. HESTON, REV. EDWARD LOUIS, C.S.C., PH.D., S.T.D., J.C.D., The Alienation of Church Property in the United States, XII-222 pp., 1941.
133. HOGAN, REV. JAMES JOHN, A.B., S.T.L., J.C.D., Judicial Advocates and Procurators, XIII-200 pp., 1941.
134. KEALY, REV. THOMAS M., A.B., LITT.B., J.C.D., Dowry of Women Religious, IX-152 pp., 1941.
135. KEENE, REV. MICHAEL JAMES, O.S.B., J.C.D., Religious Ordinaries and Canon 198, V-164 pp., 1941 (printed 1942).
136. KERIN, REV. CHARLES A., S.S., M.A., S.T.B., J.C.D., The Privation of Christian Burial, XVI-279 pp., 1941.
137. LOUIS, REV. WILLIAM FRANCIS, M.A., J.C.D., Diocesan Archives, X-101 pp., 1941.
138. MCDEVITT, REV. GILBERT JOSEPH, A.B., J.C.D., Legitimacy and Legitimation, X-247 pp., 1941.
139. MCDONOUGH, REV. THOMAS JOSEPH, A.B., J.C.D., Apostolic Administrators, X-217 pp., 1941.
140. MEIER, REV. CARL ANTHONY, A.B., J.C.D., Penal Administrative Procedure Against Negligent Pastors, XI-240 pp., 1941.
141. SCHMIDT, REV. JOHN ROGG, A.B., J.C.D., The Principles of Authentic Interpretation in Canon 17 of the Code of Canon Law, XII-331 pp., 1941.
142. SLAFKOSKY, REV. ANDREW LEONARD, A.B., J.C.D., The Canonical Episcopal Visitation of the Diocese, X-197 pp., 1941.
143. SWOBODA, REV. INNOCENT ROBERT, O.F.M., J.C.D., Ignorance in Relation to the Imputability of Delicts, IX-271 pp., 1941.
144. DUBÉ, REV. ARTHUR JOSEPH, A.B., J.C.D., The General Principles for the Reckoning of Time in Canon Law, VIII-299 pp., 1941.
145. MCBRIDE, REV. JAMES T., A.B., J.C.D., Incardination and Excardination of Seculars, XX-585 pp., 1941.
146. KRÓL, REV. JOHN T., J.C.D., The Defendant in Ecclesiastical Trials, XII-207 pp., 1942.
147. COMYNS, REV. JOSEPH J., C.SS.R., A.B., J.C.D., Papal and Episcopal Administration of Church Property, XIV-155 pp., 1942.
148. BARRY, REV. GARRETT FRANCIS, O.M.I., J.C.D., Violation of the Cloister, XII-260 pp., 1942.
149. BOLDUC, REV. GATIEN, C.S.V., A.B., S.T.L., J.C.D., Les Études dans les Religious Cléricales, VIII-155 pp., 1942.
150. BOYLE, REV. DAVID JOHN, M.A., J.C.D., The Juridic Effects of Moral Certitude on Pre-Nuptial Guarantees, XII-188 pp., 1942.
151. CANAVAN, REV. WALTER JOSEPH, M.A., LITT.D., J.C.D., The Profession of Faith, XII-143 pp., 1942.
152. DESROCHERS, REV. BRUNO, A.B., PH.L., S.T.B., J.C.D., Le Premier Concile Plénier de Québec et le Code de Droit Canonique, XIV-186 pp., 1942.

153. DILLON, REV. ROBERT EDWARD, A.B., J.C.D., Common Law Marriage, X-148 pp., 1942.
154. DODWELL, REV. EDWARD JOHN, PH.D., S.T.B., J.C.D., The Time and Place for the Celebration of Marriage, X-156 pp., 1942.
155. DONNELLAN, REV. THOMAS ANDREW, A.B., J.C.D., The Obligation of the Missa pro Populo, VII-131 pp., 1942.
156. ELTZ, REV. LOUIS ANTHONY, A.B., J.C.D., Cooperation in Crime, XII-208 pp., 1942.
157. GASS, REV. SYLVESTER FRANCIS, M.A., J.C.D., Ecclesiastical Pensions, XI-206 pp., 1942.
158. GUINIVEN, REV. JOHN JOSEPH, C.SS.R., J.C.D., The Precept of Hearing Mass, XIV-188 pp., 1942.
159. GULCZYNSKI, REV. JOHN THEOPHILUS, J.C.D., The Desecration and Violation of Churches, X-126 pp., 1942.
160. HAMMILL, REV. JOHN LEO, M.A., J.C.D., The Obligations of the Traveler According to Canon 14, VIII-204 pp., 1942.
161. HAYDT, REV. JOHN JOSEPH, A.B., J.C.D., Reserved Benefices, XI-148 pp., 1942.
162. HUSER, REV. ROGER JOHN, O.F.M., A.B., J.C.D., The Crime of Abortion in Canon Law, XII-187 pp., 1942.
163. KEARNEY, REV. FRANCIS PATRICK, A.B., S.T.L., J.C.D., The Principles of Canon Law 1127, X-162 pp., 1942.
164. LINAHEN, REV. LEO JAMES, S.T.L., J.C.D., De Absolutione Complicis in Peccato Turpi, V-114 pp., 1942.
165. MCCLOSKEY, REV. JOSEPH ALOYSIUS, A.B., J.C.D., The Subject of Ecclesiastical Law According to Canon 12, XVII-246 pp., 1942 (printed 1943).
166. O'NEILL, REV. FRANCIS JOSEPH, C.SS.R., J.C.D., The Dismissal of Religious in Temporary Vows, XIII-220 pp., 1942.
167. PRINCE, REV. JOHN EDWARD, A.B., S.T.B., J.C.D., The Diocesan Chancellor, X-136 pp., 1942.
168. RIESNER, REV. ALBERT JOSEPH, C.SS.R., J.C.D., Apostates and Fugitives from Religious Institutes, IX-168 pp., 1942.
169. STENGER, REV. JOSEPH BERNARD, J.C.D., The Mortgaging of Church Property, 186 pp., 1942.
170. WALDRON, REV. JOSEPH FRANCIS, A.B., J.C.D., The Minister of Baptism, XII-197 pp., 1942.
171. WILLETT, REV. ROBERT ALBERT, J.C.D., The Probative Value of Documents in Ecclesiastical Trials, X-124 pp., 1942.
172. WOEBER, REV. EDWARD MARTIN, M.A., J.C.D., The Interpellations, XII-161 pp., 1942.
173. BENKO, REV. MATTHEW ALOYSIUS, O.S.B., M.A., J.C.D., The Abbot *Nullius*, XVI-148 pp., 1943.
174. CHRIST, REV. JOSEPH JAMES, M.A., S.T.L., J.C.D., Dispensation from Vindicative Penalties, XIV-285 pp., 1943.
175. CLANCY, REV. PATRICK M. J., O.P., A.B., S.T.Lr., J.C.D., The Local Religious Superior, X-229 pp., 1943.

176. Clarke, Rev. Thomas James, J.C.D., Parish Societies, XII-147 pp., 1943.
177. Connolly, Rev. John Patrick, S.T.L., J.C.D., Synodical Examiners and Parish Priest Consultors, X-223 pp., 1943.
178. Drumm, Rev. William Martin, A.B., J.C.D., Hospital Chaplains, XII-175 pp., 1943.
179. Flanagan, Rev. Bernard Joseph, A.B., S.T.L., J.C.D., The Canonical Erection of Religious Houses, X-147 pp., 1943.
180. Kelleher, Rev. Stephen Joseph, A.B., S.T.B., J.C.D., Discussions with Non-Catholics: Canonical Legislation, X-93 pp., 1943.
181. Lewis, Rev. Gordian, C.P., J.C.D., Chapters in Religious Institutes, XII-169 pp., 1943.
182. Marx, Rev. Adolph, J.C.D., The Declaration of Nullity of Marriages Contracted Outside the Church, X-151 pp., 1943.
183. Matulenas, Rev. Raymond Anthony, O.S.B., A.B., J.C.D., Communication, a Source of Privileges, VII-225 pp., 1943.
184. O'Leary, Rev. Charles Gerard, C.SS.R., J.C.D., Religious Dismissed After Perpetual Profession, X-213 pp., 1943.
185. Power, Rev. Cornelius Michael, J.C.D., The Blessing of Cemeteries, XII-231 pp., 1943.
186. Shuhler, Rev. Ralph Vincent, O.S.A., J.C.D., Privileges of Religious to Absolve and Dispense, XII-195 pp., 1943.
187. Ziolkowski, Rev. Thaddeus Stanislaus, A.B., J.C.D., The Consecration and Blessing of Churches, XII-151 pp., 1943.
188. Heneghan, Rev. John Joseph, S.T.D., J.C.D., The Marriages of Unworthy Catholics: Canons 1065 and 1066, XVI-213 pp., 1944.
189. Carroll, Rev. Coleman Francis, M.A., S.T.L., J.C.L., Charitable Institutions.
190. Ciesluk, Rev. Joseph Edward, Ph.B., S.T.L., J.C.D., National Parishes in the United States, VI-178 pp., 1944.
191. Coburn, Rev. Vincent Paul, A.B., J.C.D., Marriages of Conscience, XII-172 pp., 1944.
192. Connors, Rev. Charles Paul, C.S.Sp., A.B., J.C.D., Extra-Judicial Procurators in the Code of Canon Law, X-94 pp., 1944.
193. Coyle, Rev. Paul Raymond, A.B., J.C.D., Judicial Exceptions, X-142 pp., 1944.
194. Fair, Rev. Bartholomew Francis, A.B., S.T.L., J.C.D., The Impediment of Abduction, XII-122 pp., 1944.
195. Gallagher, Rev. Thomas Raphael, O.P., A.B., S.T.Lr., J.C.D., The Examination of the Qualities of the Ordinand, X-166 pp., 1944.
196. Gannon, Rev. John Mark, S.T.L., J.C.D., The Interstices Required for the Promotion to Orders, XII-100 pp., 1944.
197. Goldsmith, Rev. J. William, B.C.S., S.T.L., J.C.D., The Competence of Church and State Over Marriages—Disputed Points, X-128 pp., 1944.

198. GOODWINE, REV. JOSEPH GERARD, A.B., S.T.B., J.C.D., The Reception of Converts, XIV-326 pp., 1944.
199. KOWALSKI, REV. ROMUALD EUGENE, O.F.M., A.B., J.C.D., Sustenance of Religious Houses of Regulars, X-174 pp., 1944.
200. MCCOY, REV. ALAN EDWARD, O.F.M., J.C.D., Force and Fear in Relation to Delictual Imputability and Penal Responsibility, XII-160 pp., 1944.
201. MCDEVITT, REV. VINCENT JOHN, PH.B., S.T.L., J.C.L., Perjury.
202. MARTIN, REV. THOMAS OWEN, PH.D., S.T.D., J.C.D., Adverse Possession, Prescription and Limitation of Actions: The Canonical "Praescriptio," XX-208 pp., 1944.
203. MIKLOSOVIC, REV. PAUL JOHN, A.B., J.C.L., Attempted Marriages and Their Consequent Juridic Effects.
204. MUNDY, REV. THOMAS MAURICE, A.B., S.T.L., J.C.D., The Union of Parishes, X-164 pp. 1944.
205. O'DEA, REV. JOHN COYLE, A.B., J.C.D., The Matrimonial Impediment of Nonage, VIII-126 pp., 1944.
206. OLALIA, REV. ALEXANDER AYSON, S.T.L., J.C.D., A Comparative Study of the Christian Constitution of States and the Constitution of the Philippine Commonwealth, XII-136 pp., 1944.
207. POISSON, REV. PIERRE-MARIE, C.S.C., A.B., PH.L., TH.L., J.C.L., Droits Patrimoniaux des Maisons et des Eglises Religieuses.
208. STADALNIKAS, REV. CASIMIR JOSEPH, M.I.C., J.C.D., Reservation of Censures, X-141 pp., 1944.
209. SULLIVAN, REV. EUGENE HENRY, S.T.L., J.C.D., Proof of the Reception of the Sacraments, X-165 pp., 1944.
210. VAUGHAN, REV. WILLIAM EDWARD, J.C.D., Constitutions for Diocesan Courts, X-200 pp., 1944.
211. PARO, REV. GINO, S.T.D., J.C.D., The Right of Papal Legation, X-221 pp., 1944 (printed 1947).
212. BALZER, REV. RALPH FRANCIS, C.P., J.C.D., The Computation of Time in a Canonical Novitiate, X-227 pp., 1945.
213. DOUGHERTY, REV. JOHN WHELAN, A.B., S.T.L., J.C.D., De Inquisitione Speciali, XII-195 pp., 1945.
214. DZIOB, REV. MICHAEL WALTER, J.C.D., The Sacred Congregation for the Oriental Church, XII-181 pp., 1945.
215. EIDENSCHINK, REV. JOHN ALBERT, O.S.B., B.A., J.C.D., The Election of Bishops in the Letters of Pope Gregory the Great, VIII-200 pp., 1945.
216. GILL, REV. NICHOLAS, C.P., J.C.D., The Spiritual Prefect in Clerical Religious Houses of Study, X-140 pp., 1945.
217. HYNES, REV. HARRY GERARD, S.T.L., J.C.D., The Privileges of Cardinals, XII-183 pp., 1945.
218. MCDEVITT, REV. GERALD VINCENT, S.T.L., J.C.D., The Renunciation of an Ecclesiastical Office, XIV-179 pp., 1945.

219. MANNING, REV. JOSEPH LEROY, J.C.D., The Free Conferral of Offices, VII-116 pp., 1945.
220. MEYER, REV. LOUIS G., O.S.B., A.B., S.T.B., J.C.D., Alms-gathering by Religious, XII-163 pp., 1945.
221. O'DONNELL, REV. CLETUS FRANCIS, M.A., J.C.D., The Marriage of Minors, XII-268 pp., 1945.
222. PRUNSKIS, REV. JOSEPH, J.C.D., Comparative Law, Ecclesiastical and Civil, in Lithuanian Concordat, X-161 pp., 1945.
223. SWEENEY, REV. FRANCIS PATRICK, C.SS.R., J.C.D., The Reduction of Clerics to the Lay State, X-199 pp., 1945.
224. VOGELPOHL, REV. HENRY JOHN, J.C.D., The Simple Impediments to Holy Orders, XVI-190 pp., 1945.
225. BROCKHAUS, REV. THOMAS AQUINAS, O.S.B., J.C.D., Religious who are known as *Conversi*, X-127 pp., 1945.
226. GRIESE, REV. ORVILLE NICHOLAS, S.T.D., J.C.D., The Marriage Contract and the Procreation of Offspring, XVI-224 pp., 1946.
227. BOUDREAUX, REV. WARREN LOUIS, J.C.D., The "*ab acatholicis nati*" of Canon 1099, § 2, XII-110 pp., 1946.
228. BOWE, REV. THOMAS JOSEPH, A.B., J.C.D., Religious Superioresses, VIII-206 pp., 1946.
229. DIEDERICHS, REV. MICHAEL FERDINAND, S.C.J., J.C.D., The Jurisdiction of the Latin Ordinaries over their Oriental Subjects, XIV-153 pp., 1946.
230. DINGMAN, REV. MAURICE JOHN, A.B., S.T.L., J.C.L., The Plaintiff in Contentious Trials.
231. FRISON, REV. BASIL, C.M.F., M.MUS., J.C.D., The Retroactivity of Law, X-221 pp., 1946.
232. CALVIN, REV. WILLIAM ANTHONY, M.A., J.C.D., The Administrative Transfer of Pastors, XII-288 pp., 1946.
233. GORACY, REV. JOSEPH C., J.C.L., The Diriment Matrimonial Impediment of Major Orders.
234. HALE, REV. JOSEPH FRANCIS, M.A., S.T.L., J.C.D., The Pastor of Burial, X-247 pp., 1946 (printed 1949).
235. HENRY, REV. JOSEPH ARTHUR, A.B., J.C.D., The Mass and Holy Communion: Interritual Law, XII-138 pp., 1946.
236. LINENBERGER, REV. HERBERT, C.PP.S., J.C.D., The False Denunciation of an Innocent Confessor, VIII-205 pp., 1946 (1949).
237. LOWRY, REV. JAMES MARTIN, A.B., J.C.D., Dispensation from Private Vows, XII-266 pp., 1946.
238. LYNCH, REV. GEORGE EDWARD, A.B., S.T.L., J.C.D., Coadjutors and Auxiliaries of Bishops, X-107 pp., 1946 (printed 1947).
239. LYNCH, REV. TIMOTHY, M.S.SS.T., J.C.D., Contracts between Bishops and Religious Congregations, XIII-232 pp., 1946.
240. McCLUNN, REV. JUSTIN DAVID, A.B., S.T.L., J.C.D., Administrative Recourse, VII-142 pp., 1946.

241. Lohmuller, Rev. Martin Nicholas, A.B., J.C.D., The Promulgation of Law, XII-140 pp., 1947.
242. McGrath, Rev. James, A.B., J.C.D., The Privilege of the Canon, XII-156 pp., 1946.
243. Marbach, Rev. Joseph Francis, A.B., J.C.D., Marriage Legislation for the Catholics of the Oriental Rites in the United States and Canada, XIV-314 pp., 1946.
244. Shimkus, Rev. Bernard Aloysius, A.B., J.C.L., The Determination and Transfer of Rite.
245. Smith, Rev. Vincent Michael, A.B., S.T.L., J.C.L., Ignorance Affecting Matrimonial Consent.
246. Wachtrle, Rev. Paul Anthony, A.B., J.C.L., The Baptism of the Children of Non-Catholics.
247. Crotty, Rev. Matthew Michael, J.C.D., The Recipient of First Holy Communion, X-142 pp., 1947.
248. Eagleton, Rev. George, J.C.D., The Quinquennial Faculties, Formula IV, XIV-199 pp., 1947 (printed 1948).
249. Gibbons, Rev. Marion Leo, C.M., J.C.L., Domicile of the Wife Unlawfully Separated from Her Husband, XIV-171 pp., 1947.
250. Kelly, Rev. Bernard M., S.T.L., J.C.D., The Functions Reserved to Pastors, XII-141 pp., 1947.
251. Kilcullen, Rev. Thomas J., LL.M., J.C.D., The Collegiate Moral Person as Party Litigant, X-150 pp., 1947.
252. Lafontaine, Rev. Germaine Joseph, W.F., J.C.D., Relations Canoniques entre le Missionaire et Ses Superieurs, X-117 pp., 1947.
253. Lane, Rev. Loras Thomas, A.B., S.T.L., J.C.D., Matrimonial Procedure in the Ordinary Court of Second Instance, XVI-184 pp., 1947.
254. Lover, Rev. James Francis, C.Ss.R., J.C.D., The Master of Novices, X-168 pp., 1947.
255. McNicholas, Rev. Timothy Joseph, J.C.D., The *Septimae Manus* Witness, XII-133 pp., 1947 (printed 1949).
256. Marositz, Rev. Joseph John, M.S.C., J.C.D., Obligations and Privileges of Religious Promoted to the Episcopal or Cardinalitial Dignities, XII-180 pp., 1947.
257. Murphy, Rev. Francis Joseph, J.C.D., Legislative Powers of the Provincial Council, XII-158 pp., 1947.
258. O'Brien, Rev. Romaeus William, O.Carm., J.C.D., The Provincial Superior in Religious Orders of Men, X-294 pp., 1947.
259. Pfaller, Rev. Benedict Anthony, O.S.B., J.C.D., *The ipso facto* Effected Dismissal of Religious, XII-225 pp., 1947.
260. Popek, Rev. Alphonse Sylvester, J.C.D., The Rights and Obligations of Metropolitans, XX-460 pp., 1947.
261. Ristuccia, Rev. Bernard Joseph, C.M., J.C.D., Quasi-Religious, XVI-318 pp., 1947 (printed 1949).
262. Sonntag, Rev. Nathaniel Louis, O.F.M.Cap., J.C.D., Censorship of Special Classes of Books, XII-147 pp., 1947.

263. Stadler, Rev. Joseph Nicholas, J.C.D., Frequent Holy Communion, X-158 pp., 1947.
264. Szal, Rev. Ignatius Joseph, J.C.D., The Communication of Catholics with Schismatics, XII-217 pp., 1947.
265. Wagner, Rev. Urban S., O.F.M., Conv., J.C.D., Parochial Substitute Vicars and Supplying Priests, IX-126 pp., 1947.
266. Quinn, Rev. Joseph, M.A., J.C.D., Documents Required for the Reception of Orders, XIV-207 pp., 1948.
267. Bennington, Rev. James Clement, A.B., J.C.L., The Recipient of Confirmation.
268. Blaher, Rev. Damian Joseph, O.F.M., A.B., J.C.D., The Ordinary Processes in Causes of Beatification and Canonization, XVI-290 pp., 1948 (printed 1949).
269. Clune, Rev. Robert Bell, B.A., J.C.D., The Judicial Interrogation of the Parties, XII-142 pp., 1948.
270. Courtemanche, Rev. Basil F., B.A., J.C.D., The Total Simulation of Matrimonial Consent, XX-120 pp., 1948.
271. Dlouhy, Rev. Maur John, O.S.B., A.B., J.C.L., The Ordination of Exempt Religious.
272. Donovan, Rev. John Thomas, Ph.B., S.T.L., J.C.D., The Clerical Obligation of Canons 138 and 140, XII-209 pp., 1948.
273. Freking, Rev. Frederick W., A.B., S.T.B., J.C.D., The Canonical Installation of Pastors, XII-210 pp., 1948.
274. Fulton, Rev. Thomas B., J.C.D., Prenuptial Investigation, XII-190 pp., 1948.
275. Godley, Rev. James P., J.C.D., Time and Place for the Celebration of Mass, X-206 pp., 1948 (printed 1949).
276. Kane, Rev. Thomas A., A.B., B.S., J.C.D., Jurisdiction of the Patriarchs of the Major Sees in Antiquity and in the Middle Ages, XII-111 pp., 1948 (printed 1949).
277. Kennedy, Rev. Andrew A., J.C.L., The Annual Pastoral Report to the Local Ordinary.
278. Konrad, Rev. Joseph George, J.C.D., Transfer of Religious to Another Community, VIII-284 pp., 1948 (printed 1949).
279. Kress, Rev. Alphonse, J.C.L., Contumacy in Ecclesiastical Trials.
280. McCartney, Rev. Marcellus Anthony, O.F.M., M.A., J.C.D., Faculties of Regular Confessors, XII-164 pp., 1948 (printed 1949).
281. McCaslin, Rev. Edward Patrick, M.A., S.T.L., J.C.L., The Division of Parishes.
282. McElroy, Rev. Francis J., A.B., J.C.L., The Privileges of Bishops.
283. Quinn, Rev. Stephen, M.S.SS.T., J.C.D., Relation Between the Local Ordinary and Religious of Diocesan Approval, XII-153 pp., 1948 (printed 1949).
284. Schneider, Rev. Edelhard Louis, S.D.S., B.A., J.C.L., The Status of Secularized Ex-Religious Clerics, X-155 pp., 1948.

285. Thompson, Chester J., A.B., J.C.L., The Simple Removal from Office.
286. O'Brien, Rev. Kenneth R., A.B., J.C.D., The Nature of Support of Diocesan Priests in the United States, XVI-162 pp., 1949.
287. Metz, Rev. John E., S.T.L., J.C.D., The Recording Judge in the Ecclesiastical Collegiate Tribunal, X-130 pp., 1949.
288. Reinhardt, Rev. Marion J., S.T.L., J.C.D., The Rogatory Commission, XIII-182 pp., 1949.
289. Ortega Uhiuk, Rev. Juan, S.J., J.C.L., De Delicto Sollicitationis.
290. Casey, Rev. James V., J.C.D., A Study of Canon 2222 § 1, XII-127 pp., 1949.
291. Allgeier, Rev. Joseph L., J.C.D., The Canonical Obligation of Preaching in Parish Churches, X-115 pp., 1949 (printed 1950).
292. Cahill, Rev. Daniel R., J.C.D., The Custody of the Holy Eucharist, XVI-178 pp., 1949 (printed 1950).
293. Carr, Rev. Aiden, O.F.M., Carm., S.T.D., J.C.L., Vocation to the Priesthood: Its Canonical Concept.
294. Knopke, Rev. Roch F., O.F.M., J.C.D., Reverential Fear in Matrimonial Cases in Asiatic Countries: Rota Cases, XII-112 pp., 1949.
295. Lavelle, Rev. Howard D., J.C.D., The Obligation of Holding Sacred Missions in Parishes, XVI-142 pp., 1949.
296. Mickells, Rev. Anthony B., J.C.L., The Constitutive Elements of Parishes.
297. Noone, Rev. John J., J.C.D., Nullity in Judicial Acts, X-147 pp., 1949 (printed 1950).
298. Sheehan, Rev. Daniel E., J.C.L., The Minister of Holy Communion.
299. Statkus, Rev. Francis J., J.C.L., The Minister of the Last Sacraments.
300. Cook, Rev. John P., J.C.D., Ecclesiastical Communities and Their Ability to Induce Legal Customs, XII-152 pp., 1949 (printed 1950).
301. Fazzalaro, Rev. Francis J., J.C.D., The Place for the Hearing of Confessions, X-150 pp., 1949 (printed 1950).
302. Hannan, Rev. Philip M., J.C.D., The Canonical Concept of *congrua sustentatio* for the Secular Clergy, XII-237 pp., 1949 (printed 1950).
303. Quinn, Rev. Hugh G., S.T.L., J.C.L., The Particular Penal Precept.
304. Gallagher, Rev. John F., J.C.L., The Matrimonial Impediment of Public Propriety.
305. Welsh, Rev. Thomas J., J.C.L., The Use of the Portable Altar.
306. Waters, Rev. Joseph L., S.S.J., J.C.L., The Probation in Societies of Quasi-Religious.
307. Regan, Rev. Michael J., J.C.L., Canon 16.
308. Byrne, Rev. Harry J., J.C.L., Investment of Church Funds.
309. Gallagher, Rev. Thomas V., J.C.L., The Rejection of Judicial Witnesses and Testimony.
310. Chatham, Rev. Josiah G., Ph.B., S.T.L., J.C.L., Force and Fear as Invalidating Marriage: the Element of Injustice, XIV-183 pp., 1950.
311. Brown, Rev. James Victor, O.R.S.A., J.C.L., The Invalidating Effects of Force, Fear, and Fraud Upon the Canonical Novitiate.

312. Duerr, Rev. Charles J., B.A., J.C.L., The Judicial Notary.
313. Gonzalez, Rev. Francisco J., O.S.A., J.C.L., De Parocho Religioso Eiusque Superiore Locali.
314. Hannon, Rev. James J., J.C.L., Holy Viaticum.
315. Sadlowski, Rev. Erwin L., J.C.L., The Sacred Furnishings of Churches.
316. Sego, Rev. Arthur A., J.C.L., Dispensation From the Interpellations.
317. Waterhouse, Rev. John M., J.C.L., The Power of the Local Ordinary to Impose a Matrimonial Ban.
318. Frein, Rev. Eugene B., J.C.L., The Discretionary Power of the Defender of the Matrimonial Bond.
319. Carton, Rev. George A., J.C.L., The Time Factor in the Gaining of Indulgences.
320. Walsh, Rev. John J., C.S.Sp., J.C.L., The Jurisdiction of the Inter-ritual Confessor in the United States and Canada.
321. Unterkoefler, Rev. Ernest L., S.T.L., J.C.L., The Presiding Judge in Matrimonial Causes of First Instance.

www.ingramcontent.com/pod-product-compliance
Lightning Source LLC
LaVergne TN
LVHW050227080826
844660LV00012B/491

* 9 7 8 0 8 1 3 2 2 4 7 5 6 *